"Mr. Dayton's book *Sing and Change the World* is informative, inspiring, well-researched, well-written—a delightful book. It is a must for every teacher's curriculum library."
—Betty Sturgess, Choir Director, Teacher of the Year, Writer of children's musicals

This book was such fun to read as I learned the origins of many familiar songs and phrases. I knew words had power to change my world. But now I know how much music empowers those words.
—Barbara Hoberman Levine, Author
Your Body Believes Every Word You Say

"*Sing And Change the World* is a must-read. It is a heartfelt book that will help children, students, teachers, parents, and business folks tackle any problems they face by breaking into song. What a neat concept. Keep this book handy, and you'll have a song in your heart always."
—Bud Gardner, Co-Author
Chicken Soup for the Writer's Soul

"This work reflects a deep understanding of and appreciation for the priceless contribution that singing makes to the human experience. Nothing lends itself better to the expression of both the joys and sorrows of life than singing. Music and song have been a constant sustaining force throughout the history of man. Hats off to David Dayton for his attempts at honoring the powers of this incredible art form."
—Cheri Murphy: Vocal Coach,
Professional Singer

"I love the book! I could not put it down. Each story got better and better! I too sing in the car on the way to work! I find that it uplifts me and puts me in a positive mood. I look over at other people driving and wonder why they aren't singing! I fully believe in the power of singing as it relates to healing of the soul, mind, body and spirit."
—Roberta Hower, RN, MSN, CCRN
Singing Nurse

To Francisca,

Sing

And Change The World

**From Davy Crocket to Princess Di,
Dozens of Voices Show You How**

by

David Edward Dayton

[signature: David Edward Dayton]

Published by

Aslan
PUBLISHING
Fairfield, CT

Aslan Publishing
2490 Black Rock Turnpike, #342
Fairfield, CT 06432
Please contact the publisher for a free catalog.
Phone: **203/372-0300**
Fax: **203/374-4766**
www.aslanpublishing.com

IMPORTANT NOTE TO READERS:

The suggestions in this book for wellness, healing and personal growth are not meant to substitute for the advice of a trained professional such as a medical doctor, social worker or psychiatrist. It is essential to consult such a professional in the case of any physical, emotional or mental symptoms. The publishers and author expressly disclaim any liability for injuries resulting from use by readers of the methods contained herein.

Library of Congress Cataloging-in-Publication Data

Dayton, David Edward.
   Sing and change the world: from Davy Crocket to Princess Di dozens of voices
show you how / by David Edward Dayton.
      p. ccm.
   ISBN 0-944031-92-7 (pkb.)
   1. Music, Influence of. 2. Singing--Social aspects. 3. Music--History and criticism.

ML3920 .D29 2002
782--dc21

                                                            2002028231

Editing and book design by Dianne Schilling
Illustrations by David Francis Dayton
and other members of the David Dayton family
Cover design by Miggs Burroughs
Printing by Baker Johnson, Inc.
Printed in the USA

To all singers, especially my wife, Karin,
and our eight children: David, Sarah, Faith,
Mary, Nathan, Patience, Hannah, Catherine.

Just start in to sing as you tackle the thing that cannot be done, and you'll do it.

—Edgar A. Guest

Patience Dayton

Acknowledgments

A finished book is rarely the result of one person's efforts. Hundreds of people contributed to the making of *Sing and Change the World,* with a bit of information here, a fact there, or an encouraging word. I am grateful to them all and to all the authors and writers who first recorded the stories I have drawn upon. Some folks, however, deserve special mention.

Thank you, Aunt Francis, for your singing story, which inspired me to start this work. Thank you, Mrs. John Duffy, the first person who ever told me I could sing. Thank you, celebrities, for taking the time to support "just another fan." Each time one of your letters arrived, I rushed back to the typewriter with a new wave of enthusiasm and hope.

Thank you, friends and family, for contributing personal letters and anecdotes about the power of singing. Thank you, friends and colleagues, for your testimonials; you know even better than I the positive impact of music and song.

Thanks to my children for contributing the art and making this book a family project. And to CSUS and Colonial Heights librarians for directing me to the best sources. Thank you, John Beltzer, for your help, support, and contacts.

Thanks to *Methodist Recorder* for copies of back issues—and to *Optimist* and *St. Anthony's Messenger* for publishing the articles that grew into this book.

Thanks to Dianne Schilling for book design and editing, Miggs Burroughs for the cover design—and to Barbara H. and Harold Levine, and Aslan, for publishing the book.

Loving thanks to my wife, Karin, for praying constantly for the success of this book.

Thank you, God, for gracing us with singing.

A few can touch the magic string
And noisy Fame is proud to win them—
Alas for those that never sing,
But die with all their music in them!

—Oliver Wendel Holmes

David Francis Dayton

Foreword

I worked as a singer for 20 years before I decided to become a teacher. In fact, singing got me through college. Unfortunately, during my first year of teaching I was diagnosed with cancer of the larynx and had my right vocal chord removed. Thanks to skillful surgeons, sufficient scar tissue formed to give my left vocal chord something against which to vibrate. This left me with a weak, scratchy, but usable voice, for which I am forever grateful. But this voice was not my singing voice. In fact, I could barely carry anything close to a tune for the first four years or so.

It took a long time to accept, and adjust to, the loss of my voice. I almost gave up music completely, but in time saw that, by giving up something I loved so much, I'd only be hurting myself. So I joined a band as a guitarist and keyboard player. We became quite popular in our local area, and wound up playing some of our city's biggest events. It was at one such event—a Fourth of July gathering—that I had a transforming experience brought about by, of all things, singing.

The band had been learning quite a few songs at rehearsals. As we were learning them, I would often "sing" into a microphone, when the lead singer was absent, just to let the horn players know where we were in the song. The band members told me that I sounded good after one particular song, and convinced me to start performing it in concerts. People did not seem to be offended by my singing, though I was never convinced that it sounded at all good.

Everyone, but me, was having a good time that July evening. I was picking apart every aspect of our performance. The horns were out of tune, the drummer's tempos were erratic, my guitar solos were terrible, and on and on. By the time we were finished, the crowd was roaring and everyone was in high spirits—even me. But once we stopped, I immediately slid back into my earlier frame of mind. I couldn't find one good thing to say or think about our band. And as I was complaining to myself about how terrible we were, a young woman came up to me. I'd met her a few times in years past so I remembered her.

She had tears in her eyes. I asked if she was all right and she said she was just fine. She wanted to tell me that she had heard what I'd gone through with my cancer experience and was deeply struck that I had persisted in singing after my surgery. She went on to confess that she had burst into tears when I began singing. She said that my continuing to sing in spite of having only one vocal chord was a real inspiration to her.

Needless to say, I was completely taken aback by this. It was one of those moments when God uses us to teach one another without our expecting it. I had been seeing only the rhythms and notes, the nuts and bolts of our performance. I was evaluating it from nothing but my own perspective. I had no idea what effect we were really having. And this young woman got to see how important it is to keep singing even when you may not think you're worth hearing anymore. You never know who's listening!

Now I have the privilege and joy of introducing this book to you. Remember my first year of teaching and how hard it was for me to accept the loss of my singing voice? Well, when I began my second year, I was at an all-time low. I had lost my singing voice and all confidence in my ability as a teacher. I also learned that I'd been moved to a kindergarten classroom—a place I hadn't been since I was five years old! Needless to say, I was not enthusiastic about my chances.

Fortunately, I was teamed in that classroom with the author of this book, David Dayton. David is a first-rate teacher and an excellent singer. He uses singing constantly in the classroom. His big bass voice appeals instantly to children, and his knack for writing a simple song with a clever lyric makes him a true asset in any educational setting. During that second year of teaching, David Dayton almost single-handedly resurrected my hopes for a teaching career. He and the children did much the same for my hopes for a singing career. David's drive, optimism, and integrity have been an inspiration to me for almost ten years now. I heartily recommend his book to any and all singers. There is something here for everyone. I pray you will enjoy the book, and follow the author's fine advice: *Sing and change the world!*

Jeffrey D. Curtis

Contents

I. Sing Your Way to a Better Day 1
Singing My Way to a Better Day 2

II. Sing and Change the World 7
Letter from Frankie Laine 8
1. Once Every 26,000 Years 9
2. The Child Who Lifted a Pillar 12
3. Song of the Dead 14
4. The Battle of the Bands 17
5. The Christmas Carol Truce 19
6. The Song and the Quake 21
7. Singing Martyrs 23
8. The Man Who Feared to Sing 25
9. Singing Themselves Into a Nation 27
10. The Song That Won the War 29
11. The Big Bad Wolf 32
12. The Coal Miner's Son 35
13. Inspired to March by Singing 38
Ten Ways to Sing and Change the World 39

III. Sing and Save a Life 41
14. A Little Old Song 42
15. The Song That Stopped a Sniper's Bullet 43
16. A Boy and His Pony 46
17. The Choir That Sang Down Death 48
18. Singing with Davy Jones 50
19. The Pope and the Plague 52
Ten Ways to Sing and Save a Life 54

IV. Sing and Find Success 58
Letter from Robert Goulet 59

20. The Singing Abolitionist 60
21. What's in a Name? 62
22. The Cowboy's Secret Weapon 65
23. The Captain and His Choir 68
24. The Four Octave Wonder 70
25. The Singing Prisoners 72
26. The Secretary Who Sang Her Way Into the Movies . . . 74
27. Baby, Take a Bow 76
28. The Throw Away Hit 78
29. The Sound of Success 80
30. A Record For Mama 82
Ten Ways to Sing and Find Success 83

V. Sing and Promote Healing 86
Letter from Catherine Dayton 87
31. Demons in the Head 88
32. The Swedish Nightingale 89
33. A Queen and a Princess 91
34. Hearts in San Francisco 94
35. The Woman of Silence 96
36. POWs 99
37. Songs of Love 102
Ten Ways to Sing and Promote Healing 104

VI. Sing and Solve a Problem 107
Letter from Merle Levy 108
38. Remember the Alamo 109
Letter from Fess Parker 112
39. The Girl Who Sang for America 113
40. Singing To Save a Dead Man 116
41. Singing For Daily Bread 117
42. Roll Out the Barrel 118
43. Just As I Am 120
44. The Song Symphony 121

45. The Devil Made Him Do It 123
46. Puritan Teenagers 124
47. The People Who Sang Up Deer 125
48. The Reluctant Bride 127
49. The Jubilee Singers 129
50. Singing in a Cave 131
Ten Ways to Sing and Solve a Problem 133

VII. Sing and Remember 135
Letter from Karin Dayton 136
51. Man Versus Machine 137
52. I've Been Working on the Railroad 139
53. A Pair of Kings 142
54. Homer's Greatest Hits 144
Ten Ways to Sing and Remember 145

VIII. Sing and See the Incredible 148
55. Clearing a Confederate's Name 149
56. General Frances E. Willard .152
57. Coffin Clocks 154
58. The Titanic and Other Disasters 156
59. The Governor Who Wrote a Song 158
60. A Sometimes Man 160
61. Cowboy on a Reindeer 162
62. Million Seller Lesson Plans .164
63. Two Worlds of Singer George Harrison 166
64. The Kansas Rocking Bird 168
Ten Ways to Sing and See the Incredible 169

IX. A Song to Get You Started 172
Author's Solo 172

Resources 177
Index 181
About the Author 189

I.

SING YOUR WAY TO A BETTER DAY

Singing to Save a Kidnapped Son

In the Alfred Hitchcock suspense thriller, *The Man Who Knew Too Much*, Doris Day and Jimmy Stewart are having a very bad day. They are a typical American family vacationing in Egypt, caught in a series of mishaps and dragged into an assassination plot. The plotters keep the couple from talking by kidnapping their son.

A very bad day.

The two worried parents pursue the plotters and their son to an embassy building and mother Doris sits down at the piano in the drawing room with a melodious plan. She sings the title song, "Que Sera, Sera," ostensibly as a recital for the guests, but puts enough energy into her voice to send the song into the upper rooms of the mansion. The hidden boy hears the familiar tune and responds by whistling as loudly as he can.

Father James tracks the whistling, breaks down the door and saves him.

Typical American parents have saved their son by singing a song. Now they can

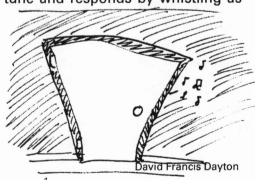

David Francis Dayton

go about having a better day.

Can singing give you a better day?

Here is my own story as evidence....

Singing My Way to a Better Day

If you can walk, you can dance. If you can talk, you can sing.
—Zimbabwe Proverb

Several years ago as I stood on a cold bathroom floor, the glass medicine cabinet shelf crashed behind the mirror. The blue ceiling paint peeled down, straining to touch the torn shower curtain. I stepped into the stall and stared at a battalion of ants marching across the upper border of blue-green tiles. A daddy long-legs dropped down from his corner web and caught a red victim. The cement around the faucet cracked and leaked sand.  The white grout wheezed holes. And the drywall under the tile was mostly dry rot.

But King David the Psalmist sang, "Forever I will sing the goodness of the Lord."

And Roman poet Horace wrote, "Gloomy cares will be lightened by song."

And William James the psychologist said, "I don't sing because I'm happy; I'm happy because I sing."

So instead of grumbling, complaining, or giving up, I sang.

Today, the bathroom has been fixed, but my approach to each new set of twenty-four hours is still the same.

I sing.

I sing my way to a better day.

I used to hear the alarm and groan. Now I sit up and judge my mood. Am I gloomy, grouchy, or glum? If so, I take the advice of professional singer Kathy Elzey who says, "Singing is more than a physical rush. It's emotional and cathartic. Even singing sad songs makes me feel good—I get the sadness out." If you wake up with the Monday morning blahs, quietly sing a sad song and purge them out.

In the shower I am ready to wake up and belt out. But I never belt out too soon. Veteran singer Jeff Curtis suggests, "Always warm up before you start hitting it hard—don't strain yourself. Use long tones with the vowel sounds: a, e, i, o, u. It's very similar to exercise. It's all about breath control."

I roll the long vowels out of my mouth. The tones bounce off the ceiling, fly out the bathroom window, and cause our dog, Kaiser, to whine back through the screen. The howl rolls in with some nippy morning air. It's time to wake up, wash, and warble.

Singing loud in the shower deepens breathing, relaxes the body, and lowers blood pressure. Hold those notes as long as possible and reap the benefits of better oxygen intake with more energy. Some might like the mental stimulation of Gilbert and Sullivan's "A Modern Major General," or the rolling appeal of Rogers and Hammerstein's "Oklahoma," but I explode in my shower with the strident tones of "Amazing Grace" and "The Battle Hymn of the Republic." Sing what you love and you will love to sing.

"The psychological benefits are half the battle," says cardiopulmonary technologist H. Gordon Kemnitz. "Singing is a very controlled activity. It will wake you up and keep you awake."

As you get out of the shower to dry, now is the time to set your mind for the day. I have my own positive song, which combines Norman Vincent Peale's favorite Bible verses, advice from a great salesman, and my own singing experience. The melody is of my own making—a simple chant that has sent me off to success.

If God be for us, who can be against us?

I can do all things through Christ who strengthens me.

Do what you fear and you'll conquer your fear.

Sing your way to a better day.

Find those personal statements about life that energize your hopes and dreams, attach them to a tune or rhythm, and set your mind on a positive note while you pat your body dry.

As I get dressed, I cut my morning voice. Waking others into a bad mood while singing myself into a good mood is contrary to charity. Worse, my wife might throw a shoe at me.

Kathy Elzey has a solution: "You can always hum or sing in your head. Besides keeping the peace, humming is a good break from full-voice singing. It keeps you from drying out your throat."

Springing into my car, I key the ignition and start down the block with one of three options: I sing a song of faith if I still fear my day, I sing an American standard if I am feeling fine, or I break into a bit of musical nonsense if my mind is giddy with energy and optimism.

Signal lights blink, carbon monoxide blows, traffic jams, but singing in my car blows the city smudge away. Removed from road rage and the noise of the street, I go with a glow.

Reaching the final turns, I switch into something that grows with a rising melody like "America the Beautiful" or "God Bless America." A song peak will push my soul up to a mountain high. The surge of energy will be greatest when it follows the surge of passion in the chorus. The best part of a song helps me carry my best attitude into the day. Make the moment you leave your car to go into the workplace a crescendo, not a low note.

Hum your favorite tunes as you go about your duties. Let the sound clear your head and shield your heart from the drudgery and petty annoyances of life.

I teach Kindergarten children at Bowling Green School

in Sacramento. I can sing all day and they love it. We sing hello. We sing the calendar. We sing the names of the students who are present. We sing our poems, we sing our books, we sing for music time.

We sing directions to the groups. I sing at the table *voce sotto* (in a low voice), but the children two feet away can hear and they laugh.

"You are funny, Mr. Dayton."

"Yes," I agree, "and happy."

I inherited my humor and happiness from my Aunt Francis. She stood up behind her office desk one afternoon and announced, "What this place needs is a good song!"

To the astonishment of all the other employees, Aunt Fran broke forth with, "Down by the old mill stream!"

"Take the second verse, Edna!" Fran directed. Edna did. So did Marge. Soon everybody in the department joined in and kept the refrain rolling. When the boss opened the door and walked into that wall of sound...well, my Aunt Fran will long be remembered.

Adults need music, too. I sing around the school frequently. Special occasions, celebrations, faculty meetings, retirements, staff parties—all call for a song.

I have sung for other schools in workshop presentations. I have sung for the school board to plead for Bowling Green needs. I have even crooned at California State Senate hearings on education. Put your business into a song! People listen when you sing. Professionals, politicians, and the press all take note.

If I have a bad experience at work, I reflect on it in my car and sing a sad song to purge it as I travel, so it will not impede my attitude at home.

Once home, I sing some more.

How did all the singing start?

Blame my Dodge Dart. No radio. From eighteen on I filled the car with my own *a cappella* songs about stop signs, pedestrians, destinations, and what-not.

Married with babies made the singing practical. My wife, Karin, and I discovered that a chorus of "I've Been Working On the Railroad" calms down a crying infant—at least long enough to get home.

The singing habit stuck. I sang everywhere. Not always for the public, but often in public. I sang security shift. I sang for college assignments. I sang for children's birthday parties.

Now I sing without control.

I sing in the bathroom—"I need a washcloth to take my bath!" I sing at the dinner table, "Pasta! Pasta! Eat it when it's hot!" I sing for general purposes—"Everybody get into the car!"

I sing on the phone, on special occasions, on not-so-special occasions. Singing is a medium through which any number of wonderful things can be accomplished.

Now my children sing and their successes have expanded the singing arena even further. They sing to pass tests; they sing to cheer up friends; they sing to deal with exceptional problems.

No matter how many you have in your house or how well they sing, you can be a singing example if you sing, whistle or hum light and happy as the day draws to a close.

Then out with the light and fall asleep. Never sing while you sleep. Snore if you must, but let the vocal apparatus take a rest. Wait till tomorrow to wake with a song in your heart, ready to sing your way to a better day.

Convinced?

Yes or no, turn to the rest of the book and be inspired by kings, queens, presidents, paupers, saints and sinners who have sung and made history before you. Then you, too, might sing and change the world.

II.
SING AND CHANGE THE WORLD

The Beatles Sing to Save Pepperland

In the 1960s cartoon film *Yellow Submarine*, the Beatles sing many songs. Each song introduces a character or celebrates the fun of zipping underwater in a yellow submarine. The spirit of joy stops, however, when the Beatles reach Pepperland, and see a world given over to gloom. The Blue Meanies have put the cold finger upon the inhabitants and want to "blue" them in with eternal despair.

How do the Beatles save Pepperland?

They sing another song.

An animated John Lennon bursts forth with the anthem of the decade, a song introduced in the world's first continent-to-continent satellite hook-up—

"All You Need Is Love."

The song blasts back the Blue Meanie monsters and fills the land with dandelions, violets, and daisies. The warm song of flower power and

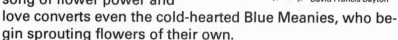
David Francis Dayton

love converts even the cold-hearted Blue Meanies, who begin sprouting flowers of their own.

Singing a song saves a cartoon world.

Can singing change the flesh and blood world?

Here are Saint Augustine, King Richard the Lion-Hearted, Civil War General Daniel Butterfield, and civil rights marcher Sheyann Webb to prove it can. But first, a letter from world-acclaimed singer Frankie Laine with an anecdote about singing's power to heal and testimony to singing's power to impact the world in which we live.

NOVEMBER 14, 2000

DEAR DAVID,

MY DEAREST MEMORY OF HOW A SIMPLE SONG CAN TOUCH PEOPLE OCCURRED DURING THE 1954 TOUR OF ENGLAND. THE COMMAND PERFORMANCE WAS AN INCREDIBLE PROFESSIONAL THRILL, BUT THE PERSONAL HIGHLIGHT FOR ME WAS THE TIME I SPENT WITH A LITTLE SIX-YEAR-OLD GIRL NAMED JEAN HANCOX. HER FEET WERE AMPUTATED AFTER A STREET CAR ACCIDENT, AND FOR A WHILE THE DOCTORS FEARED FOR HER LIFE. THEY GAVE HER ARTIFICIAL LIMBS, AND LEARNING TO WALK ON THEM WAS A TRAUMATIC ORDEAL FOR HER. WHILE SHE WAS CONVALESCING SHE WOULD LISTEN TO FRANKIE LAINE TIME, A SHOW THAT WAS BROADCAST OVER RADIO LUXEMBOURG. SHE WROTE TO TELL ME THAT MY SONGS (PARTICULARLY HER FAVORITE, "WILD GOOSE") HAD HELPED HER TO FORGET HER PAIN.

EACH YEAR I FREELY DONATE SEVERAL CONCERTS TO MY COMMUNITY. I LOVE SINGING AND I LOVE THIS GIFT TO MY COMMUNITY. FROM THE THOUSANDS WHO ATTEND, FROM THE LETTERS AND REMARKS TO ME, AND THE GENERAL FEEDBACK, I FEEL, GRATEFULLY, THAT THIS GIFT OF SONG HAS BEEN A GRAND HELP IN THE COMMUNITY—LOVE REFLECTING LOVE.

GOD BLESS,

Frankie Laine

1. Once Every 26,000 Years (c. 1850)

Awake and sing, ye that dwell in dust.
—Isaiah

Up in the heavens sparkles a star whose position never changes, but once every 26,000 years.

Polaris, the "permanent" North Star is located at the handle end of the Little Dipper. American slaves taught their children to locate Polaris by finding the Drinking Gourd (Big Dipper) and the two stars at the end of the bowl. Drawing an imaginary straight line from the bottom star through the top star and continuing straight across the sky led the observer to the critical North Star. To "Follow the Drinking Gourd" and head north was the first step in finding freedom.

By 1860 slaves made up one-third of the population of the South. Most worked picking cotton—men and women breaking their backs in the field. They cleared land, planted seed, and harvested crops. Teenagers worked with adults. Children pulled weeds, carried water, and learned the location of the North Star.

Men, women, and children lodged in wooden huts, on naked earth. No furniture. No bedsteads. Slaves slept on straw and rags with a single blanket. Other rags plugged the cracks in the timbered walls, but wind, rain, and snow still swept in. Water soaked the ground until the floor resembled a pig sty.

One fireplace, many families. Modesty dropped a few pegs. Young men slept in the kitchen. Young women slept with their parents. Some families tried to partition off sections for privacy.

Children wore nothing but a shirt. Older ones sported a pair of pants or a gown. In winter, a jacket. A pair of shoes once a year.

Meals consisted of cooked corn meal, herrings, and vegetables raised by the slave's family on a truck-patch. When the food ran short, the slaves would steal to eat. Breakfast at twelve, supper at twilight, and late at night the children learned to locate the North Star.

Imagine life as a slave. You are a piece of property—an expensive piece, but property no less. You may not stay outside after dark. You may not gather in a group. You may not leave your owner's land without a written pass. You may not own a weapon. You may not learn to read or write.

You have no family. You may be married, but your marriage is not recognized. You may have children, but they can be taken away.

You may meet together with grandparents, parents, aunts, uncles, and cousins in the precious time away from work, but do not deceive yourself. Tomorrow you could be sold down the river, and never see them again.

So, from early on, you learn the position of the North Star. And to guide you to freedom, you memorize a song.

When the sun comes back

And the first quail calls,

Follow the Drinking Gourd.

For the old man is awaiting to carry you to freedom

If you follow the Drinking Gourd.

In late winter or early spring, look at the Big Dipper—the Drinking Gourd—and find Polaris, the North Star, to guide you in the right direction to freedom. The Underground Railroad will send you an "old man" to guide and conduct you into the free states.

The riverbank makes a very good road,

The dead trees will show you the way,

Left foot, peg foot, traveling on,

Follow the Drinking Gourd.

Slaves escaping in the eastern states have many routes available to freedom, but you are in the Deep South and must start your escape on the banks of the Tombigbee River, which flows through Alabama. Dead trees hold markings that distinguish the direction you are to go each time another river or creek flows into the Tombigbee, forming a 'Y.' Always, always, you follow the North Star.

The river ends between two hills,

Follow the Drinking Gourd.

There's another river on the other side,

Follow the Drinking Gourd.

The Tennessee River runs over the hills from the Tombigbee. Climb those hills and switch rivers, continuing on, always north, following the North Star.

When the great big river meets the little river

Follow the drinking gourd,

For the old man is awaiting for to carry you to freedom

If you follow the Drinking Gourd.

When the Tennessee meets the Ohio—the Big River, you will cross over and meet the "old man" guide. The Ohio is no small swim. At one time the Underground Railroad advised all slaves to escape in winter and cross the great Ohio by striding over its frozen ice. You must look for a canoe, a raft, or chance a floating log.

Wet and dripping, you are on the free side of the great Ohio. Walk stealthily still. The laws of the nation are not kind to a slave. You could be returned and severely punished. But perhaps you will be fortunate and find your "old man" guide who will lead you to ultimate freedom.

Polaris—the North Star—will continue in position for 26,000 years. Thanks to "Following the Drinking Gourd," your slavery will not. A song has helped you survive to freedom.

HARMONIOUS FACT: How did slaves born into an Orwellian world of no news, no knowledge, and no outside vision, conceive of escape? Frederick Douglas first decided to flee from bondage when he heard fellow slaves singing "Run to Jesus; shun the danger!" Ex-slaves such as Douglas added fuel to the antislavery fire, moving the country forward into the Civil War and the eventual abolition of slavery.

---

2. The Child Who Lifted a Pillar (c. 386)

The song on its mighty pinions, took every living soul,
and lifted it gently to heaven.
—Longfellow

A boy danced down a Roman road and sang a simple song,

Tolle lege! Tolle lege!

Familiar nursery rhyme words to most children of the Roman world. Plain nonsense to most grown-ups. He moved along the road and came to one of the high white walls of a Roman aristocrat, a wealthy man who could afford high white walls to surround his garden. The walls kept out the riffraff. But no wall, no matter how high, could keep out a song.

Tolle lege! Tolle lege!

The boy's song sailed over the white wall and aroused the sunken body of public speaker and acclaimed orator Augustine of Hippo.

Once the pinnacle of society, Augustine now wanted off the pedestal. The man who once held Carthage in his palm now wished to cast the city aside. Augustine, the worldly, desired to break with the world. But he feared his own weakness. He feared relapse. He feared building the walls of a towering new life and not being able to complete the task. How could he be sure he would succeed?

Tolle lege! Tolle lege!

The boy's singing awoke the weary Augustine. "Tolle lege? Take up and read?" He reached out to a volume of St. Paul's Epistles lying on the grass under the tree. He prodded the book open with a finger and, following the dictates of the song, read at random, "Put on the Lord Jesus Christ and make no provision for the flesh."

The verse lifted the weight of the world off the ex-libertine's shoulders. Years of delight in loose living, sinful consolation, and pampering the heart dissolved into the dust. Grace flooded his soul. He wrapped himself up in his savior and believed he could succeed. The child's song echoed from far down the street.

Tolle lege! Tolle lege!

Straight as a column stood the once-crumpled August-ine. He strode into the house and sought his long-suffering mother, Monica. He fell at her feet. He wept. He apologized for his wasted life. And he told her his miracle of redemption.

Tolle lege! Tolle lege!

Next, the pinnacle of renewed strength marched off to friend, mentor, and holy bishop St. Ambrose to make full confession for his life. Ambrose smiled with joy and asked for an account of the transformation.

Tolle lege! Tolle lege!

The humbled but hope-filled Augustine entered the Church, freed from his burden of doubt. A vocation awaited. He became a priest to live as Christ. He wrote to conquer temptation. He spoke to vanquish the heresies he once embraced. He told his story to all who would listen.

Tolle lege! Tolle lege!

In a few short years, the people christened Augustine successor bishop by popular demand. His philosophic work would lay the foundation for Christian theology for nearly one thousand years. Proclaimed a doctor by the pope, he proved himself a pillar of the Church. A pillar lifted up into place by one boy singing a song.

Tolle lege! Tolle lege!

HARMONIOUS FACT: How did a future English mayor find his vocation? Dick Whittington ran away from his servant position after a beating by the cook. While sitting on the outskirts of London, he heard the bells sing to him, "Return Dick Whittington, thrice Lord Mayor of London!" He returned, grew up, and prospered as a merchant. And just as the singing bells prophesied, he reigned thrice as Lord Mayor of London in the 1300's.

---

3. The Song of the Dead (c. 1860)

Arms and the man I sing.
—Virgil

General Daniel Butterfield heard the shots fire again. Not the bullets of a battle, or the explosions of a charge, or even the firecracker noise of a surprised skirmish. These shots rang out in the dead of night when both armies had settled in and gone to sleep.

A sergeant and several men hurried up to the general's tent and reported the awkward news.

"They did it again, sir."

"Again?" muttered the general.

"Yes, sir," continued the sergeant. "Shall I dispatch another detail?"

"Yes!" thundered the General, then reversed himself. "No." Caught in a dilemma, the distinguished recipient of the Medal of Honor decided to give himself some time to think.

The sergeant saluted and returned to his duty—watching over the fallen who could not be buried.

"Every time I send out a detail to lay those men to rest," grumbled the General to his orderly, "those blasted Confederates try to lay the detail to rest."

"It's the salute, sir," said the orderly. "When the detail fires the gun salute, the rebels take it as an attack."

"Yes," sighed the General. He had led many live men into battle, but now he was stumped leading dead men into their graves.

Assuming the General needed time alone, the orderly excused himself with a few words. "Goodnight, sir."

"Goodnight?" echoed the General. The phrase lit up his mind with a solution. "That's it! Call my bugler."

The orderly rushed out of the tent and sought out the bugler, an Oliver W. Norton. The bugler hurried into the Commanding Officers tent, brandishing his golden horn. "We need a song," said the General. "Something appropriate for a funeral. A plain dirge to give dignity to the fallen in place of the normal rifle volleys. And I have it."

Oliver W. Norton stood in his commanding officer's tent and listened to the General whistle a tune, a smooth, slow melody the bugler recognized as adapted from a harsh official piece dubbed "Tattoo."

"Play that for me," requested the General.

Mr. Norton lifted his bugle to his lips and for the first time in any war, the swansong of all wars lifted its melody up to heaven and graced the camp with the peace of a day now done.

"Exactly," smiled the General. "Get that sergeant back in here and we'll send the detail out once more."

The perplexed sergeant returned.

"Take the bugler with you," commanded the General. "Instead of giving a gun salute, he will play a farewell over the graves."

The farewell song worked. The Confederates left the burial detail alone. "Butterfield's Lullaby," as it became known throughout the Civil War, served not only as a goodbye to a fallen comrade, but as a popular alternative to the current "Lights Out" as a signal that day was done, reflected most strongly in the song's words:

Day is done, gone the sun,

From the lake, from the hills, from the sky.

All is well, safely rest, God is nigh.

Retitled "Taps," the general's tune caught on as the Army's foremost ceremonial song and made it possible for hundreds of Union burial teams to serve their dead comrades without dying in the process.

General Daniel Butterfield saved men through valor and strategic command. But he saved even more lives by singing and writing a song. A song that stopped war on the battlefield long enough to bury the dead.

HARMONIOUS FACT: How do people throughout the world handle the grief of death? They sing burial songs. In the Potlatch Ceremony of upper northwest North America, the men sing "sorry songs" — spontaneous expressions of grief—that chronicle the life of the deceased and release the emotional pain of those involved.

4. Battle of the Bands (c. 1860)

Two people can sing together but not speak together.
—German proverb

America's Civil War set brother against brother. On the eve of the War Between the States, many families discovered that geographical accidents of birth split the family loyalties and sent sons off to separate armies and opposing causes. Something stronger than politics, however, remained in the gray and blue uniformed boys in the field. In spite of war, that something would rise up again when called forth by a song.

In Northern Georgia, after several years of the national "family feud," two legions confronted each other, put up camp, and rested for the night. But even after laying down their bayonets, the sibling soldiers could not resist carrying on the fight.

At eight p.m. the Union army band struck up Francis Scott Key's "The Star-Spangled Banner." The Confederates responded with the Southern anthem "Dixie." Union brass volleyed back the dignified "Hail Columbia." The Confederates fired off the Christmas carol tuned "Maryland, My Maryland." Union fifes whistled the primeval "Yankee Doodle." Confederates cannonaded "Bonnie Blue Flag." The Union bass thundered the apocalyptic "Battle Hymn of the Republic."

Then came a pause.

A brief silence entertained the stars and cold sky over Georgia. The men in blue smiled at each other. Nothing could outplay the Battle Hymn; it was God's own song meant to hammer the South into submission.

The Southern army conceded the battle in the realm of brass and bass drum, but the Southern band still had one more song to play. Something not quite martial, but still fiercely patriotic.

A fresh refrain shot up to the moon and warmed the night. The Union musicians listened puzzled, then wept. Raising their instruments once more, they played, not to overwhelm the enemy, but to harmonize with them.

Soldiers on both sides dropped their guns. Tears fell as mouths opened and ten thousand voices echoed over the battlefield with one united refrain:

Be it ever so humble, there's no place like home.

Something more than politics remained in the brothers: love of home. Singing a shared song brought the armies of the blue and the gray back into one family again as America's bloodiest war stopped one night for the sentiment of a popular song.

HARMONIOUS FACT: How can Catholics, Baptists, Lutherans, and all manner of Christian denominations find ecumenical common ground? They may argue and debate doctrine or theology, but they have no trouble singing a good hymn together; ecumenism among believers can begin with a song.

---

5. The Christmas Carol Truce (c. 1914)

*As long as men continue to struggle for a better world,
they will need songs to encourage them in that struggle.*
—Edith Fowke and Joe Glazer

Sing and change the world? It has happened.

June 28, 1914, an assassin gunned down Archduke Francis Ferdinand of Austria-Hungary in Sarajevo. The killer, Gavrilo Princip, worked with a terrorist group in Serbia. Austria-Hungary blamed Serbia for the assassination and declared war.

A system of military alliances pulled all the major European powers into the fight. Most expected quick victory. Most received lingering destruction. Ten million troops would die. Emperors would fall.

The peace settlement would create conditions leading to Adolf Hitler, the Holocaust, and World War II. World War I would direct and delineate the course of the twentieth century—one hundred years of the millenium's worst armed destruction and militant slaughter.

In December of 1914, the Germans and the British ordered their million-man armies to dig a line of trenches across Belgium and northeastern France. The soldiers blackened the ice with bombs, gunpowder, and blood.

But then came December 24, 1914, and the stroke of midnight. A trickle of song rose from the German side of the line.

Stille Nacht, heilige nacht.

The British answered back.

All is calm. All is bright.

The two mud-caked armies joined each other in carols over the bleeding trenches. The miracle expanded. Soldiers laid down their bayonets, set aside their pistols, and called a Christmas truce. The singing led to sharing cigarettes and brandy, and playing soccer in no man's land by the light of the flares.

The "war to end all wars" stopped. The battle that would open the door to continental slaughter took a recess. The fight to reconfigure the world, which would set the stage for another Armageddon culminating in the fission bombing of Hiroshima and Nagasaki, paused for a song.

Then came the end of Christmas. And the end of singing. The fighting resumed. One million British and two million German dead.

As one commentator noted, "One wishes that they could have gone on singing." Even so, for one day, a song made good the promise of Christmas for peace on earth, and temporarily timed out world war.

Sing and stop a massacre. Sing and change the world.

HARMONIOUS FACT: How did Franz Gruber and Joseph Mohr solve the problem of a broken-down organ and subsequent loss of music for Christmas mass? Franz began strumming his guitar; within a short time, he devised the melody for the world's most beloved Christmas carol—"Silent Night." He shared the tune with Father Joseph who pulled a set of appropriate lyrics out of his drawer, which he had written years before. The song not only "saved" Christmas mass, it later rose up over the trenches to suspend world war and "save" Christmas in 1914.

---

6. The Song and the Quake (35 A.D.)

Sing praise to the Lord with all your hearts.
—St. Paul Ephesians 5:19

Paul and Silas wanted no trouble, but what could they do? What could two grown men do when a possessed girl followed them everywhere they walked and hollered and shrieked? Not once, not twice, but for three days straight?

"Keep your temper, Paul," warned Silas. "We don't want to make any trouble with the authorities. We've only been in Philippi a week."

But Paul had reached his limit. He stopped, turned, stared at the slave girl and said, "In the name of the Lord Jesus Christ, I command you to come out of her."

The spirit possessing the girl vanished and the girl collapsed. The slave's owners waxed furious. They had been making good money from their spirited fortune-teller.

"Seize those men!" shouted the Phillipian business associates. "They are Jews and they're advocating illegal practices!"

The Roman soldiers took Paul and Silas into custody for disrupting the marketplace and put them into prison to stand charges for proselytizing. To assure maximum security, the jailer chained his prisoners' feet to a stake.

Other prisoners must have been surprised to see these two erudite gentlemen thrust into the darkest cell among them and bolted to the stones of the floor. Thieves or murderers—certainly. Mild-mannered Jews? What could these men have done to deserve such treatment?

The prisoners soon received their second shock of the evening. Instead of grumbling outrage or quietly dying into the dark, the fledgling convicts began to sing. Silas and Paul treated their fellow inmates to a round of hymns.

Some prisoners may have drifted off to a peaceful rest as the disciples kept praising God in melodies old and new and improvised. Others may have listened throughout the night, contemplating the verses and the attitude of two remarkable men. Both kinds of prisoners—sleepers and listeners—would soon experience their third shock.

At midnight, at the height of the singing, a severe earthquake rocked the prison. Doors flew open and chains pulled loose.

The Roman jailer panicked, pulled his sword and prepared to end his own life. (By law, jailers were held accountable to suffer the punishments of escapees.) He placed the tip of the sword upon his breast and prepared to fall upon it into death.

"Don't kill yourself," shouted Paul, "we are all here."

The jailer held up his lamp and checked the prison. Only the two singers stood free from the chains, and the two singers made no attempt to escape. The jailer fell to his knees in thanksgiving, converted to Christianity on the spot, and escorted his singing convicts to his own home to celebrate his conversion.

The next morning, the authorities dropped the charges and sent Paul and Silas on their way to continue singing and spreading their faith.

HARMONIOUS FACT: Some historians call it a legend; others say it might well have happened. During the Crusades, an enemy ruler imprisoned the returning King Richard the Lion-Hearted. His location was discovered by his minstrel who wandered through Europe singing. When Richard heard his minstrel put forth the first verse of a song the king himself had composed, he rejoined from the dungeon with the chorus. One of the first instances of a songwriter saving himself with his own song.

---

7. Singing Martyrs (c. 203)

Song is untouched by death.
—Ovid

In Rome stands one of the most famous ruins in the world. Four stories tall, the oval Colosseum is about one hundred fifty feet high, six hundred feet long, and five hundred feet wide. The massive structure of brick and concrete is decorated in columns and arches, and held forty-five thousand spectators.

Emperor Vespasian began construction after sixy-nine A.D. His successor dedicated the arena in the year eighty. With awnings over the fourth floor to protect the audience from the sun and rain, and eighty entrances for easy patron access, the Colosseum made a perfect theater for mock naval battles, gladiator combat, and fights to the death between wild beasts and confessed Christians.

One such Christian was Perpetua.

Perpetua converted to Christianity against her pagan father's wishes and found herself condemned to death under the Emperor Septimus Severus. Septimus followed a tradition of persecution begun by Nero, but saw the growing number of Christians in his century to be a threat against the republic. He increased the penalties for conversion, directed officials to seek out Christians in their districts, and raised the executions to a new high. Suddenly, the Colosseum and its arena counterparts around the Roman Mediterranean received a staggering infusion of victims for spectacles. Perpetua's martydom is not the only story, but it is a prime example of God and faith using singing to convert mangling death into miraculous witness.

Here is what the crowd in the amphitheater saw.

Two animal handlers jammed a spear into a pen containing a leopard, causing it to snarl and snap back at the bars. The two rough men gave similar treatment to a wild bear. Finally, the wicked duo set upon a caged boar. When all three beasts reached peak ferocity, the "trainers" called for the condemned and set the beasts free.

Two Christian men walked out first. Without shield, spear, or armor, they swiftly fell before the angered animals. The crowd roared with bloodlust and cried for more victims.

Now Death called for a holy woman. Trainers brought in a heifer with sharpened horns. They whipped it into a butting frenzy.

"Out with the Christian!" cried the crowd.

Out came lady Perpetua—singing.

The crowd sat puzzled. What kind of lunatic was this woman?

Perpetua sang a song of praise. Some moment in the middle of the song, the heifer made its charge and plunged a sharp horn into her abdomen. The crowd raised its voice to cheer...then stopped.

Perpetua kept singing. She never saw the heifer. She never experienced the goring. She began singing and kept singing, caught up in a prayerful singing ecstasy.

The officials quickly removed the embarrassment from their amphitheater; the Captain of the prison guard sent out a Roman soldier to dispatch Perpetua with a knife.

For three hundred years, that is what the crowd would see until the Roman Empire converted into the Holy Roman Empire under the emperor Constantine. Then the Colosseum would become an abandoned piece of ancient architecture, giving up its stones to buildings for the Medieval age. But that would be three hundred years later.

Meanwhile, out came more singing martyrs, spreading their faith with their lives, their deaths, and their songs.

HARMONIOUS FACT: How did a group of Danish Jewish women prisoners preserve their sanity and their souls as their concentration camp tormentors annihilated their bodies with starvation and persecution? They recalled the suffering of the slaves in America and sang the slave spiritual "Steal Away" to steal away their minds from the pains of the present and endure the horror of their evil captivity.

---

8. The Man Who Feared to Sing (c. 680)

God ...gives songs in the night.
—Job 35:10

Some people are afraid to sing.

Whenever Caedmon heard a refrain, he rose up and ran for his life. A good Englishman, he loved to join in with friends at a feast. But the custom after dinner terrified him. The host would rise, seize a silver-stringed harp, and break forth with the beginning stanza of a rousing ballad. Then the hand-held instrument moved to a guest who sang out another original verse, relinquished the lyre, and challenged his neighbor to surpass it. Caedmon never waited for the harp to get too close.

One evening, the spotlight-shunning man escaped the medieval version of karaoke by rushing off to a stable where he held charge of the cattle. Caedmon collapsed in the yellow hay, but his sleeping relief soon ended. God had a song to sing. Call it a dream, a vision, or an encore of Balaam's donkey (see Numbers 22:28), Caedmon experienced something unusual in the manger that night. One of the heifers spoke up, making the unpardonable demand.

"Caedmon," cried a piebald cow, "sing me something."

"I cannot," lamented the half-asleep Caedmon. "I left the dining hall and escaped here because I could not sing."

"Nevertheless," said the forthright beast, "you can sing for me."

"What shall I sing?" stalled the rising Caedmon, eyeing the barn door.

"Sing about creation," suggested the creature.

Straightaway, Caedmon burst into spontaneous song, singing verses in praise of God the Creator, verses of a song he had never heard before. Then he fell asleep—or continued dreaming.

The next morning, Caedmon shared his story with several friends. Everyone smiled at his miraculous tale until they heard him sing. Then they were astonished. The man too afraid to sing contained a voice which surpassed all others. He delighted his friends and all listeners with his sudden ability to versify and sing any passage of Scripture or Church doctrine with melodious abandon.

Whatever the cause or nature of his conversation with the cow, his singing gift from God proved sensational. The local abbess—the discerning St. Hilda of Whitby—advised him to leave the world, take the vows of religion, and learn the entire course of sacred history.

The inspired troubador humbly obeyed and broke out on a canticle binge. Each piece of knowledge his teachers put in came caroling back out of Caedmon's mouth as a song. He sang the whole story of Genesis (with several lyrics on cows), the flight of Israel out of Egypt, and the history of the Promised Land. Moving to the New Testament, he sang the incarnation, passion, and resurrection of Jesus, the Holy Spirit's descent, and the works of the apostles. He rounded out Revelation with a hymn of heaven's joys and a dirge about the sorrows of hell.

Caedmon never quit singing.

He traveled the English countryside in a time when preachers were scarce and printed books unknown. The psalms welling up out of his own being continued to draw others to God and instruct them in the faith.

Some say the English still intone holy verses attributed to the man too afraid to sing, brought into his vocation of spreading the faith by the gift of a song.

HARMONIOUS FACT: How can children who are not afraid to sing overcome other fears with a song? A nine-year-old boy learned to cope with a school phobia by singing calming lyrics as he approached the classroom; the singing made it possible for him to adjust to a new environment. Preschoolers have successfully dealt with separation anxiety by listening and singing along with recordings of their parents singing favorite songs.

---

9. Singing Themselves Into a Nation (c. 1781)

I celebrate myself, and sing myself.
—Walt Whitman

Be careful whom you mock—even in a song.

Dr. Richard Shuckburgh laughed at the poorly dressed colonial troops who joined the British regulars to fight in the French and Indian War. Even as he dressed their wounds, the physician swelled with the urge to poke fun at the so-called soldiers who left woods and farm to fight for the crown.

In a spare moment, the doctor took an English ditty and improvised some nonsense lyrics to taunt the colonials. The British soldiers later embraced the mockery and sang the joke with gusto, even deriding the colonists on Sunday by standing outside church windows and outsinging the hymns.

The colonials did not like the mockery. They did not like a lot of other things as well—among them the Stamp Tax, the Tea Tax, and the Intolerable Acts. So they began taking steps toward revolution. And one of those steps was to learn Dr. Shuckburg's song.

Suddenly, the British troops found themselves fighting an enemy who could hide anywhere, strike without warning, and sang back their mockery as a battle cry. The Yankee Doodles of derision now became the Yankee Doodles of decision. And the Yankee Doodles were so unfair about it.

Yankee Doodle went to town riding on a pony.

Stuck a feather in his hat and called it macaroni.

But Yankee Doodle did not ride into town on a pony. He stayed out in the woods where he could not be seen. He stuck no feathers in his hat to make himself visible. He stuck balls of lead into his musket and mowed down fine British soldiers.

And there was Captain Washington upon a slapping stallion,

And giving orders to his men, I guess there was a million.

And who was this military commander, Washington? Who did he think he was crossing the river and fighting on

Christmas? No honor among these colonialists! Not even among their commissioned officers.

"Yankee Doodle" played in every patriot camp and colonial soldiers whistled it in battle. The British heard the tune so much and so often, General Gage exclaimed, "I hope I shall never hear that tune again!" as he directed the retreat from Concord.

Many things conspired to give the final victory to the Americans. Credit George Washington, friends in parliament, guerrilla warfare, and foreign powers. But the Yankees gave a good measure of credit to their fighting spirit fueled to the burning point by a particular song.

If there is any doubt about the power of one song to uphold a nation in the hour of its greatest need, the colonials removed the doubt during the surrender of Lord Charles Cornwallis to General George Washington on Oct. 19, 1781. While the British band sadly played "The World Turned Upside Down," the Continental Army trilled out "Yankee Doodle," the song Americans sang to win the war, to make themselves a nation, and to change the world.

HARMONIOUS FACT: How did the tenant farmers of New York State revolt against abusive landowners? They donned Indian disguises and sang a parody of "Old Dan Tucker," a popular song. They sang until they sang their way to victory; legislation passed in their favor and the feudal system was abolished.

---

10. The Song That Won the War (c. 1860s)

The song that nerves a nation's heart is in itself a deed.
—Tennyson

Once upon a time upon the Italian peninsula, two Greek colonies found themselves at odds. Materialistic Sybaris and idealistic Croton could not live together without an uncivil war.

How did this come about?

Well, the philosopher Pythagorus lived among the Crotoniates and gained converts to his anti-materialistic, anti-Sybaris way of life. The converts converted the whole city and the whole city set itself against Sybaris—the symbol and cradle of evil.

But Sybaris was a power to be reckoned with. With three times as many soldiers, they set upon Croton first with their own set of complaints. Too late, the city of Croton realized its doom. Three hundred thousand soldiers and calvary marched upon the defenders of Croton on a spring day in the year 510 B.C.

The Crotoniates cried to Pythagorus, and Pythagorus came up with a last minute salvation. He collected a band of musicians and sent them ahead to meet the Sybarite cavalry at the Crati River.

Sybaris loved its horses and trained them to march in spectacular parades. The horses would pirouette, prance, get up on their hide legs, and do any number of tricks. The horses did all their dancing to a song.

As the Sybarite cavalry moved forward to invade, Pythagorus directed the musicians to lift their instruments and play the Sybarite marching tune.

The horses responded and the calvary fell into confusion. The Crotonian army marched forward to destroy and conquer.

The city of Croton won its uncivil war with a song.

A couple millenia later, another Civil War is in process among the inheritors of the Greek democracy. The United

States is no longer united as the South and the North do battle. Right now, with superior generals, the South has the upper hand.

The Confederates hold their heads high after almost a solid week of victory. The Union soldiers crawl out of their bunks, wounded and bruised. Common sense would call the war off. The Union boys can not stand up to the rebels and their tactics. But just as defeat seems imminent, something comes into the Northern camp, a weapon of power and inspiration.

Yes, we'll rally round the flag, boys,

We'll rally once again,

Shouting the battle cry of Freedom,

We will rally from the hillside,

We'll gather from the plain,

Shouting the battle cry of Freedom!

Soldiers begin singing the song. At first, a couple. Then a squadron. Finally the whole troop. The voices grow and shake the air and infuse the soldiers with hope. Better than a furlough. Better than a victory. The Union army resurrected. Singing "The Battle Cry of Freedom" recharges the troops and sends an electric chorus across the enemy lines.

A Confederate Major listening from the other side observes in his diary, "Here we've licked them six days running and on the seventh they're singing! Sounds like the knell of doom!"

We are springing to the call

Of our brothers gone before,

Shouting the battle cry of Freedom;

And we'll fill our vacant ranks with

A million free men more,

Shouting the battle cry of Freedom.

The Civil War period has been dubbed the "singingest war" in American history. Whereas the colonials relied heavily upon "Yankee Doodle," the two sides of the War Between the States composed and played an entire repertoire of songs.

The South rallied behind "Bonnie Blue Flag" and the joyous "Dixie." The North started even before the war with abolitionist soul-stirrer "John Brown's Body." When the war began, they unleashed the historical and traditional favorites "Star-Spangled Banner" and "Yankee Doodle."

But in the battle of the bands, the North had even more melodic ammunition to ignite.

Julia Ward Howe witnessed the Union army in review singing the popular "John Brown's Body" and sat down to write even more soul-shaking lyrics. Her words appeared in the *Atlantic Monthly* as "The Battle Hymn of the Republic" and thundered over the South as a victory march.

Union army bandmaster Patrick Gilmore put together "When Johnny Comes Marching Home," giving the North the prediction of victory with every verse sung.

Then George F. Root wrote "The Battle Cry of Freedom," the keynote song of the Northern effort to persevere and succeed. The song topped all Union tunes in its power to inspire, motivate, and endure.

This time, a song did more than throw horses into a mad dance; it threw a wild desire into the North to win. The Union army refused to quit. One song recruited soldiers, transformed recruits into unquenchable fighters, and carried the Union army to victory.

When the South surrendered, Abraham Lincoln played "Dixie," declaring it "an acquired spoil of war." Then he ordered the band to play "The Battle Cry of Freedom," and called it "the song that won the war."

Two armies in history saved by a song.

HARMONIOUS FACT: How did the abolitionists arouse sympathy for their cause before the war? *Uncle Tom's Cabin*, in print and on stage did much, but just as much sympathy sprang up from the singing of the anti-slavery song, "Darling Nelly Gray."

---

11. The Big Bad Wolf (c. 1933)

If I had a song, I'd sing it in the morning,
I'd sing it in the evening. All over this land.
—Pete Seeger

An old expression talks about "The wolf at your door." In the 1930s, the wolf bayed at the world's door.

Runaway inflation ruined the money in Germany, brought down the government, and crowned Hitler king. Japan tried to relieve its economic woes by invading China. In America, on Wall Street, millionaires jumped out of windows. The average citizen looked at the upper class coming down, watched the "Okies" moving out, and wondered how the country was going to get by on no employment, no money, and no hope.

Farms failed, factories failed and banks failed. Millions lost their life savings, their homes, their dignity, and turned to the government or charities for food. Once-successful businessmen hid their faces in the relief line so no one would recognize them.

More than 200,000 young people traveled the country seeking the necessities of life. Malnutrition led to death from disease. Relatives moved in together. Others built shacks out of crates to replace repossessed houses.

Food prices dropped, but no one could afford to buy. Dairymen poured milk out into the street. Stark survival became the norm as people ate from garbage cans and stole food.

Under the national umbrella of despair, an artist followed his vision. Tough times meant little to him.

As a child, Walt Disney had delivered papers in the morning cold to supplement the family income. After studying art at sixteen and working for the Kansas City Film Ad Company at nineteen, the young animator set up his own studio and found fortune in 1928 with the release of his Mickey Mouse sound cartoons.

What he never guessed was the impact one single Disney effort would have on the Great Depression.

With the addition of color and a more sophisticated re-cording system, Disney released his Silly Symphonies se-ries. His first color cartoon, *Flowers and Trees,* won an award. His second changed the hearts of 100 million Americans.

Future animator Marc Davis saw the record-breaking Silly Symphony when it first came out in 1933. He summed up the power of one cartoon with a very influential song in a letter to a fan:

"My father took me to see it at the Alhambra Theater in Sacramento. The evening shows were more expensive, and my father didn't have much money then, so he and I went to see it for 25 cents at a matinee! The film, with its song, 'Who's Afraid of the Big Bad Wolf' gave everybody such a lift in the Great Depression. It certainly left a big impression with me. It gave the world a shot in the arm when it needed it the most, and that is something I will never forget."

Audiences agreed with Mr. Davis. Suddenly, the Depres-sion became synonymous with the Big Bad Wolf. And if the Three Little Pigs could beat the wolf, then the nation could beat the Depression. The song became a rallying cry with its contemptuous "Who's Afraid of the Big Bad Wolf?" and en-couraging take-action statements, "punch him in the nose...kick him in the shin."

The same year brought a change in government and governmental policies. The country was ready to take a punch at the "big bad wolf." The Civilian Conservation Corps (es-tablished in 1933) employed thousands in conservation projects. The Federal Emergency Relief Administration (founded the same year) gave states money for the needy. The Agricultural Adjustment Administration (1933) helped regulate farm production. The National Recovery Adminis-tration (1933) set up and enforced rules of fair practice for business and industry. The Public Works Administration (1933) provided jobs in the construction of bridges, dams, and schools. The Federal Deposit Insurance Corporation (1933) insured bank deposits.

Families started gardens, raised cows, pigs, and chick-ens. People with less made do with less and appreciated what they had. Those with jobs began to realize that with prices down, the standard of living for some actually improved. The Great Depression would not end until the increased production of World War II, but in the meantime, the country's attitude had been saved by an artist, a cartoon— and a song.

HARMONIOUS FACT: How did rural families of the 1930s cope with the Depression? They sang "Can the Circle Be Unbroken?" at funerals to sustain themselves through tough times and the death of loved ones.

12. Coal Miner's Son (c. 1950)

Because the road was steep and long
And through a dark and lonely land,
God set upon my lips a song
And put a lantern in my hand.
—Joyce Kilmer

Union leaders work to improve the quality of life for thousands of workers. Union leaders use strikes, politics, and bargaining to seek their ends. But Mr. Travis changed the quality of life for hundreds of thousands of workers without strikes, politics, or bargaining.

He did it by singing a song.

Mr. Travis, a banjo-picking tobacco farmer, moved his family to Ebenezer, Kentucky and dug himself into the deep, dark hole of a coal mine. When music and smoking no longer pay, black coal always will.

The North American Indians burned Kentucky coal first. White settlers tried it, but preferred to hack down the forests and burn sweet-smelling Kentucky wood. Then the Industrial Revolution erupted with steamships and steam-powered railroads screaming for coal to fire their boilers, and the settled whites descended into the earth.

Mr. Travis returned home each night choking black, complaining, "Another day older and deeper in debt." Mr. Travis' growing debt came from the company store, owned by the coal company and designed to steal back the little the miners received for their work. Poisonous gas, falling rocks, and cave-ins caused a number of miners pain and consternation, but the mining company tortured thousands more, one day at a time, by paying them with inflated store coupons instead of cash.

The company-issued coupons redeemed only company-owned rental housing or the company-owned store goods. In both cases, the prices ran high and the miners ended up more "in the hole" living in their homes at night than working in the mines by day.

Modern machinery improved worker efficiency, but not

worker safety. By the 1950s, a miner employed in the continuous mining method could dig two tons of coal an hour, resulting in a sixteen-ton day. Increased efficiency increased risks. More miners are killed in accidents with machinery than in any other kind of mining accident.

None of Mr. Travis's misery escaped the attention of his four-year-old son. Young Merle Travis planned to be a songwriter; he stored each ache, anecdote, and complaint in the tunnels of his mind for later use. Young Travis chose to follow in his father's banjo-picking, not coal-digging footsteps.

Two friendly coal-miners—Mose Rager and Ike Everly (father of the Everly Brothers)—taught Young Travis how to use his thumb to play the bass strings on a guitar while plucking out the melody on treble strings. Escaping the dark holes of Kentucky, Young Travis hitched around the country, developing his skills as a street entertainer.

In 1935, the singing, guitar-playing Travis joined the Tennessee Tomcats, moved up to the Clayton McMichen's Georgia Wildcats, and finally became a member of the Drifting Pioneers. His talents for songwriting also paid off. He arranged "Muskrat" for Tex Ritter, which later developed into a hit single for the aforementioned Everly Brothers. Then the ascending Merle Travis dug back into the tunnels of his mind to write a tune based on his father's life in the coal mines.

With a haunting reed-wind solo, a relentless drum rhythm, and the deliberate finger-snapping of singer Tennessee Ernie Ford (he snapped to keep the beat), the Kentucky miner saga "Sixteen Tons" sold one million copies, changing coal into gold.

Merle Travis called his story about the miner "with one fist of iron and the other of steel" a "fun song," but the popularity of the country ballad raised the consciousness of the nation.

News reporters delved into the hell hole conditions of the miners and revealed to the public how major coal companies had long taken advantage of the workers. Everything from mine ventilation, to miner's wages, to black lung disease came under scrutiny and led to major reforms in the coal mining industry.

In father Travis's days, a five- to fifteen-percent mixture of naturally occurring methane gas in the air could result in a violent reaction. Federal law now requires all underground mines to have automatic methane detectors to prevent accidental explosions.

In father Travis's days, a chunk of coal ranging from the size of a dinner plate to the length of a city bus could fall and flatten a man walking between the "ribs" of a tunnel. Worse, the roof or ribs of the walls could fail and collapse, burying all workers in the area. Federal law now requires fresh mines to have scientific roof or support plans to prevent roof or rib failures leading to cave-ins.

In father Travis's day, nearly four miners in every thousand were killed in mine accidents annually. Thanks to reforms and added safety precautions, today's annual death rate has dropped more than seventy-five percent.

Banjo-picking and tobacco farming could not keep Mr. Travis out of the Depression-era coal mines of Kentucky. But his words echoing in his son's musical tribute encouraged reforms that made a difference for coal miners decades later.

Thanks to public investigation motivated by Merle Travis's "Sixteen Tons," the dignity, health and lives of many thousands of today's coal miners have been saved—by a song.

HARMONIOUS FACT: How did families of mining disaster victims survive? In the 1930s, mining tragedies were written up as ballads and sold. The proceeds from the songs went to the families of the deceased workers.

---

13. Inspired to March by Singing (c. 1965)

I sing what is in my heart. My only thought now
is to sing as I have never sung before.
—Betty Robbins

Sheyann Webb saw clubs and blood. Sheyann Webb breathed tear gas. Sheyann Webb watched police throw sixty people into jail in the spring of 1965, in Selma, Alabama, and almost became inmate sixty-one. But the nimble Southern girl escaped and ran for home, worn-out, tired, and scared by violent reactions to the protest march planned for the next day.

"The last thing I remember that day as I left the city hall and walked home," she told journalist Frank Sikora, "was the sound of those people inside—some of them were singing, 'Woke up this mornin' with my mind stayed on freedom.'"

Sheyann reached home and dropped on her bed. Through her window, again she heard singing. Men and women had gathered together to pray and prepare for the march. They sang in the evening, in the church, and the choir of voices rolled out along the fields and into the homes.

The singing of the people in prison blended with the singing of the people in church and gave the eight-year-old courage. Sheyann decided, "If they could sing, then I could go on marching."

She did march—with Dr. Martin Luther King—in Selma, Alabama, and into history. She joined Civil Rights marchers off to change the world, thanks to inspiration from neighbors singing a song.

How did the Civil Rights movement spread?

Members credit the songs which rocketed the news of the movement across the country through spirituals and common lyrics.

Civil Rights activists sang when they met. Civil Rights activists sang when they marched. Civil Rights activists sang when oppressed, threatened, and beaten. Singing gave activists the strength to endure and the method to recruit others to their cause.

Sing and support your cause.

Sing and change the country.

Sing and change the world.

HARMONIOUS FACT: the European nations watched in amazement as the Civil Rights movement led by Dr. Martin Luther King changed segregation policies and racist laws from one end of the United States to the other. The Europeans watched in amazement not because Dr. Martin Luther King spoke eloquently—many other world leaders spoke well on behalf of their causes. Not because Civil Rights protestors used nonviolence—Gandhi and his followers used nonviolence to free India from the British. They watched in amazement because the movement relied in large part on singing to carry its message, to protest injustice, to communicate its goals, and to bring about change. The movement used singing to change the nation. And all of Europe recognized the power of a song.

TEN WAYS TO SING AND CHANGE THE WORLD

1. Anthropologists believe prehistoric people, lacking a common language, might have communicated by singing. Next time you meet a world traveler of another tongue, consider using a song to communicate. *Sing and communicate better with the world.*

2. Mormons composed and sang, "Come, Come Ye Saints," to help them survive their trip to Utah and settle Salt Lake City. *Sing and complete your historic mission.*

3. Tony Pastor sang, "What's the Matter with Hewitt?" and enabled Abram S. Hewitt to win the local mayoral race. Alfred E. Smith supporters sang "The Sidewalks of New York" to elect him governor. Republicans sang Eisenhower into the White House with "I Like Ike." *Sing and support your favorite politicians.*

4. Joe Hill supported the Industrial Workers of the World by singing their goals to the union members; he believed a pamphlet would be read once, but a song would be remembered forever. *Sing and inspire others to change social conditions.*

5. John Newton wrote "Amazing Grace" in thanksgiving for his conversion to God. Millions of others have been drawn into faith thanks to a hymn or religious refrain. *Sing and bring the world to belief.*

6. Marines sang, "Smoke on the Water," to keep up their morale especially during the kamikaze raids. Opera singer Lyuba Levitsky

sang to support Jews in the ghetto. Concentration camp prisoners kept up their morale during the war years under the harsh and hopeless conditions of the Nazi taskmasters by singing an underground song called, "The Peatbog Soldiers." ***Sing to keep up morale when the world is going down.***

7. The song, "Arthur Murray Taught Me Dancing in a Hurry," made his name and method household words. Mary Kay of cosmetics fame started her Monday sales meetings off with songs; the sales force sang, sold, and made her name synonymous with success. ***Sing your business and it may cover the world.***

8. At a three-day rally in Tokyo during the '80s, John Sebastian, Jackson Browne, Richie Havens, and other performers paid Arion's debt to the dolphin by singing a benefit concert that raised $150,000 to save whales, dolphins and other sea mammals from the nets of the international fishing industry. ***Sing and save the world's ocean mammals.***

9. Willie Nelson organized the first Farm Aid concert in 1985. Since then, millions have been raised by singing for the economically strapped farmers. Sing and support our nation's food producers. Moesha's Sheryl Lee Ralph raised her voice to sing at an AIDS benefit. Opera singer Esperian sang to raise money for St. Jude Children's Research Hospital. ***Sing and raise money for world charities.***

10. Antwoine Palmer's Unity Choir changes lives by getting teenagers off the streets and into the discipline of song. Dr. Rano S. Bofill, "The Singing Doctor," travels across the country to entertain the elderly in nursing homes by conducting sing-alongs. ***Sing and make the world a better place for the young and old.***

Sing to Change the World

(Sung to "Anchors Aweigh")

Sing songs with other faiths.

Sing to change the world.

Sing to defy oppression.

Sing to change a U.N. session.

Sing to make history.

Sing to stop a war.

Sing to undo any famine.

Sing to change conditions of the poor.

III.
SING AND SAVE A LIFE

The Psychopath in the Sandbox

In the movie *Con Air*, a six-year-old girl sits in a splintered sandbox with a psychopath. There is only one thing in the psychopath's mind—how can I add Miss Freckles to my list of victims? But there are many things in the girl's mind—dolls, tea parties, and a song.

She sings.

He's got the whole world in his hands.

The psychopath sits on the edge of the sandbox enthralled. She coaxes him to join in.

He's got the whole world in his hands.

He sings, abandons his schemes, and leaves. Miss Freckles has saved her life by singing. Can singing save someone's life? Can singing save your life?

Here are Pope Gregory, a Civil War sentry, and a submarine crew to prove it can. But first, a story by Yoko Ono about her mother.

David Francis Dayton

14. A Little Old Song (c. 1998)

One day, a couple of years ago, I called my mother in Tokyo, and found her having a slight slur in her speech. It was very unlike her. I asked what was happening, and she told me that she fell on the floor in her room and did not know what happened to her. The phone on the floor rang, so she picked it up and heard me on the other end. She said in a very soft voice, "It's very strange, Yoko. I don't seem to be able to get up."

I asked her to stay still while I had my assistant call a family doctor in Tokyo from another phone. My mother kept wanting to go to sleep. Somehow, my instinct told me that she would not wake up again if she had gone to sleep then. I kept talking to her, encouraging her to engage in conversation with me. But she was sounding faint and drowsy.

Out of desperation, I proposed to sing a song to her. "Mommy, remember this song?" It was an old pop song my mother used to sing around the house when we lived in San Francisco in the 30s. "I want you to sing with me."

It was clear that my mother was suddenly feeling better. She sang slowly, gradually getting more strength in her voice. We kept singing until help came to take her to the hospital. The little old song saved her.

copyright © 2000 by yoko ono

HARMONIOUS FACT: Two Lancaster teenagers were recently kidnapped from an area about an hour north of Los Angeles. In the August 19, 2002, issue of *People Magazine,* the two girls revealed how they handled their ordeal in the back of a white Ford Bronco: Said Jacque Marris, "We knew how worried our parents, family and friends would be, and we felt awful. I started to softly sing "Blessed" and stroke Tamara's leg and arms. I always sing when I'm mad or in trouble. It's a comfort." Tamara Brooks added, "It was like my mom singing a lullaby to me. I started to sing all these songs to myself in my head. We were starting to relax a little and focus on what was going on." The two then made plans, attacked their kidnapper while he slept, and were eventually rescued.

---

15. The Song That Stopped a Sniper's Bullet (c. 1864)

Black care shall be lessened by sweet song.
—Horace

There are two sides to every story.

But in the Civil War, the soldier's life of Johnny Reb and Billy Yank ran much the same. Despite a variety of occupations, ages, and appearances, the three million American soldiers who wore the blue of the North or the gray of the South shared an amazing set of characteristics.

The typical Civil War soldier came fresh from the family farm with three years of formal education between his ears. He filled his homesick letters with "wuz" and "thar" and a hundred phonetic renderings of his daily speech with little or no punctuation.

In those letters, the soldiers complained about the heat of summer and the cold of winter, the drilling and the marching, the distaste for army ways and the distaste for army rations.

Outside of those letters, the soldiers sought comfort in the righteousness of their cause and the solace of their faith. A rifle-toting believer in the field could not always get to a church nor into a Bible, but he could open up his heart any time of the day in a hymn.

One night, one Union soldier opened his heart up in a hymn...and closed it to a sniper's ball of lead.

A Confederate commander had detailed one of his sharp-eyed farm boys to sneak up on the rival camp and put down the sentry with a single shot. The recruit followed orders as usual, slipped up through the brush, and found his exposed target looking up at the heavens rather than out at the enemy lines.

He cocked his gun and took aim, ready to dispose of the Union man with a snap of the trigger. Then he stopped cold. The Union man was singing.

Cover my defenseless head with the shadow of Thy wing.

The sniper recognized the hymn and through the song beheld a man who shared his faith, if not his politics. He suddenly found it impossible to carry out his orders.

Returning to camp, the farmer-soldier took his abasement for failure and excused himself the best he could with complaints about the darkness and the sly camouflage tricks of the Yankees.

The war ended.

The Confederate soldier returned home.

He grew his crop, grew old, retired. Then, as things would have it, he found himself in the company of old soldiers at a reunion. The group numbered equal parts Union and Confederate. They did what old soldiers do best—they swapped war stories.

The Confederate sniper told his tale. He admitted what had been in his heart that night in the brush when he had set his sights on the sentry and prepared to pull the trigger. "I couldn't kill that man," he told the soldiers, "though he were ten times my enemy."

A Union soldier spoke up. "Was that in the Atlanta campaign of '64?"

"Yes," came the reply.

The Union soldier stared at his Confederate counterpart. He remembered the night he stood his company's most dangerous post. He recalled his lonely depression, and savored the words he had sung on duty for comfort and mercy,

Reach me out Thy gracious hand!

While I of Thy strength receive,

Hoping against hope I stand

Dying, and behold I live.

Then he looked at the soldier who heeded his song and affirmed, "I was the sentry!"

A sentry saved by a song.

HARMONIOUS FACT: Samuel Craig, born in 1757, was first Lieutenant in the Company of Captain Orr. He and five other captives of the Indians were made to sit on a log awaiting execution. Samuel broke out in song and kept singing. As he sang, his poor, quiet comrades were struck down by tomahawks. The loud and entertaining singing Lieutenant, however, was spared. He was exchanged as a prisoner of war and returned to his family.

HARMONIOUS FACT: Several years ago, musician James (Jimmy) Twyman, inspired by St. Francis of Assisi, took to the road singing of peace and happiness to whomever would listen. Shortly before leaving on a European tour, Jimmy was given a copy of the peace prayers from twelve major religions. He was inspired, as he read them, and the music started to flow. By the end of the day, Jimmy had written music for each of the twelve prayers and knew there was something special about them. He has since traveled to trouble spots around the world (Bosnia, Croatia, Israel, Ireland, Baghdad and more), often risking his life to teach, sing and perform peace concerts. At his workshops and concerts in the U.S. and abroad, Jimmy teaches practical ways we can all bring more peace into our lives.

16. A Boy and His Pony (c. 1925)

Song is untouched by death.
—Ovid

Eric Kinworthy (a teenage boy) and Captain (his pony) descended into hell (an English coal mine) to stretch the family dollars by dragging tubs of loose coal packed from the coal mine's face and carting the tubs out for so many pence. He kept the miners supplied with empty tubs and gently drove his young horse down into the black hole and back out into the light several times a day. Eric rarely needed to speak to the well-trained pony, but one day he decided to sing—and singing saved their lives.

On that day, Eric led his horse down the sloping tunnel to its heart where the recent coal had been blasted, picked from the bed, and tumbled into tubs. By the light of the kerosene lanterns, Eric hoisted the tubs upon his pony's cart and then gave the horse a pat to encourage it up the slope. But a pony weighted down with coal is not anxious to go anywhere. A long afternoon of such trips had worn it down. Yet the beast staggered forth with the bones of the underworld behind its back for one more haul.

Halfway up the slope, Eric noticed the light fading at the tunnel's entrance, signaling the onset of twilight. He wanted to escape before tunnel and sky blurred into a haze of black. But the slope rose even higher up towards the mouth of the cave and the worn-down pony plodded slower not faster.

That day God inspired Eric to sing. The boy thought back to his last Sunday in church and pulled out of his memory a familiar hymn,

God moves in a mysterious way His wonders to perform.

The pony responded to the singing by clip-clopping double-time. Perhaps the horse felt a premonition as well, or maybe the surprise echos of his master's voice jolted him into action. In either case, he trotted ahead with extra vigor and the team met the twilight sooner, not later. Eric and Captain reached the end of the tunnel just as the boy sang the final notes of his song.

"Suddenly, there was an awful crash," recalls Eric. "We were jerked to a standstill. It was impossible to see anything until the dust cleared. In a little while, I found the roof had caved in and resting on top of the first two tubs was a huge stone weighing about two hundredweights. Other big stones were lying around. I was badly frightened, but realized my life had been wonderfully spared from death or certain injury. If the pony had not increased his pace a moment or two before, nothing could have saved us."

Singing a prayerful petition saved the boy and his pony. At the original pace, both might have been crushed by the collapsed ceiling stones. Thanks to an inspired song, the perked-up pony made it out with his load two seconds before the collapse.

Eric knelt in the dust and dedicated his life to God. He grew up to become a minister and told his story in *The Methodist Recorder* in December of 1946.

Captain, the perked up pony, lived out his days on an English farm.

HARMONIOUS FACT: Dear Abby's column for October 21, 2001, shared a life-changing anecdote about tormented Carol whose high school life was a nightmare. Peers laughed at her clothes and treated her with contempt. One particularly rotten day, she slipped home from school early, walked into the garage and looked for something poisonous to swallow. She turned on an old radio, cried, and found a bottle of termite poison. Just as she had worked up the nerve to use it, the radio played Dolly Parton's "Coat of Many Colors," a song that mirrored her life. She stopped cold and decided, "If Dolly made it, so can I." Today Carol is a successful college graduate, with a loving family, who works with disadvantaged kids in her spare time.

17. The Choir That Sang Down Death (c. 1677)

Singing promotes cooperation and brotherly love.
—Dr. Edward Podolsky

Allessandro Stradella must have loved his choir because he wrote so many beautiful oratorios—religious songs—for them. And the choir must have loved their composer because they sang one and saved his life.

All the troubles started because Allessandro loved something besides his choir. He loved another man's fiancée. He loved her so much, he ran away with her, she leaving her intended at the altar.

The intended—a Venetian senator—did not appreciate Stradella's theft. Not only did the senator miss his bride-to-be, he also felt outraged. Who did Stradella think he was? How dare he insult a Venetian senator!

On Stradella's behalf, it should be pointed out that he never meant to run off with the bride-to-be. At least, it was not his original plan. He had no original plan. He was a choir master and only trying to make a living. Senator Grimani had discovered a young and pretty singer, Ortensia, whom he felt could benefit from his patronage. Grimani introduced Ortensia to Stradella and paid for singing lessons.

Ortensia came up with the elopement plan. She suggested Allessandro run off with her. Allessandro foolishly agreed.

In the manner of the time, the disturbed Venetian senator hired two professional killers to hunt down and murder the lovestruck composer. A tidy piece of revenge would heal his pride, and possibly recover his future wife.

The composer and the singer made a rapid escape into the countryside of Venice. The killers followed. The couple sought help from an old friend who sent them to Rome. There Stradella composed an oratorio concerning the dance of Salome before Herod. Ortensia took the role of Salome. The killers, slow but steady, finally uncovered their trail and arrived in Rome in time for the oratorio's premiere in the church of San Giovanni of Fiorentini in 1675.

The hit men discovered Allessandro, and chased him to a stage door. But when the killers entered the theatre, they walked into the midst of the choir practicing the recently-composed Allessandro oratorio. The beauty of the singing overwhelmed them.

The hardened assassins stayed for the entire work.

The choir's song changed their hearts.

The smitten cutthroats broke their contract with the Venetian senator. Who could kill a man who wrote such wonderful music as this?

Ortensia returned to her senator with the hired killers.

Allessandro continued to write oratorios for the choir he loved so well.

Unfortunately, he also continued to run off with other men's fiancées, until one set of assassins finally did him in.

Yet, once upon a time, one choir singing one of his songs saved his life.

HARMONIOUS FACT: Faye Sidorsky collects and sings traditional Jewish songs, and is particularly dedicated to saving those songs she feels are at risk of being lost. Her grandmother, Eva Davis, was also a singer. According to Sidorsky, grandmother Davis survived Auschwitz by singing for her life. She gained extra soup one day, or a crust of bread another, by entertaining the Nazi officers. "I sing to keep these songs alive," says Sidorsky. "My grandmother sang to survive."

---

18. Singing with Davy Jones (c. 1939)

*It is a great thing in a sailor to know how to sing well,
for he gets a great name by it from the officers,
and a good deal of popularity among his shipmates.*
—Herman Melville

The Helgoland Bight is a knot of water twisting between Helgoland Island and the shore of northwestern Germany. In the early days of World War II, England decided the location would be perfect to spy on the movements of the German navy and practice sinking German ships. London military command gave the orders and an assembly-line submarine zipped through the North Sea to settle at the bottom of the Bight.

Unfortunately, once the ship settled, it stayed put.

Raw machines often come with quirks and kinks. But few machines announce their mechanical troubles at the bottom of the sea. The surprise malfunction generated a mad scramble to examine the controls, but the malfunction also shut down the lights, making the examination impossible.

The English sub had sunk itself.

The alarmed engineers roamed the engine room with flashlights, but failed to identify the fault. Whatever lever needed lifting or button needed pushing, no one could find it.

The lieutenant in charge collected the crew around him and admitted the situation appeared hopeless. He dispensed an opiate apiece to make death easier. Falling asleep seemed more agreeable than smothering in the dark.

Then one man touched by religious devotion broke the stale air with the words of a well-known hymn. Others joined in and the verses of "Abide with Me" soothed the men better than the drugs.

Singing with a vanishing oxygen supply turned out to be the worst—and best— thing to do. Several verses into the hymn, one of the more vigorous vocalists lost his breath and passed out. His fainting body fell into a corner and struck a hidden lever.

Lights flashed, gears cranked, and the submarine hummed to life. Engineers manned their posts and the commander called out to resurface. The singing resulted in a reactivated submarine and twenty-odd overjoyed crew members.

The happy sailors rose up out of the cold waters of the North Sea and thanked God for their resurrected ship. The song they thought would send them through the pearly gates saved them from a salty grave.

HARMONIOUS FACT: A group of medieval bandits found themselves trapped in a house and surrounded by enemies even less scrupulous than themselves. The danger caused a change of heart in the trapped men. They cried out to their home patron, St. Columba, and began singing hymns begging his intercession. The suddenly devout and harmonious gang members successfully escaped through the rival gang's flames, swords and spears, losing only those among them who refused to sing.

---

19. The Pope and the Plague (c. 604)

He who sings frightens away his ills.
—Miguel de Cervantes

A little bacterium can be a dangerous thing.

In the 1300s a germ called *Yersinia pestis* swept through Europe inside the stomachs of fleas on the backs of rats. The rats traveled from seaport to seaport with the fleas passing pestilence along to all humans within biting distance.

Humans became overcome with nausea, aches and pains. Then followed the swelling of the lymph glands around the neck, under the arms, and along the groin. Finally red spots of blood under the skin turned black, resulting in extinction and the plague's name: The Black Death.

The epidemic began in China and spread quickly to Europe. One quarter of the continent's people died. Further outbreaks over the next few centuries continued to decimate populations in Europe until the late 1600s when the disease contained itself. No doctor, no physician, no king, no queen could contain it. But seven hundred years earlier, in 604, a pope put a stop to a similar outbreak of the bubonic by leading his people in singing.

Pope Gregory liked music, especially singing. He liked it so much that he spent a good portion of his papal effort increasing the use of plainsong in the Church liturgy. He may not have invented the musical form, but he promoted it so well that it bears his name even today.

Gregorian Chant—the sound of dozens of voices following a tune built on modes or scales with carefully rising and falling melodies. Spiritual music. Music to pray by and rest the soul by. So melodious today that the fourteen-hundred-year-old song form is making a comeback not only in the Church but on the popular music charts.

But Pope Gregory had other things to do besides encourage singing. He put on the papal mantle in a city given over to an outbreak of the plague.

The streets of Rome in the earlier Middle Ages suffered from occasional overflows from the river Tiber. The water brought with it the perfect conditions for disease. Gregory took authority during one of these severe outbreaks; he became Pope in a city of death.

How does a Pope stop the plague? Pope Gregory organized the people to sing. From seven great churches in Rome proceeded seven great columns of Christians in a processional litany beginning at St. Mary Major. "Sing out!" exhorted Gregory and the people chanted "Kyrie eleison" even as the dying fell about them. Moving up the water-pocked streets, tramping through pools of wet infestation, the faithful sang. "Kyrie eleison!" for the bodies. "Kyrie eleison!" for the souls. "Kyrie eleison!" for the departed. "Kyrie eleison!" for the half-dead. Three days of death march with Gregory in the streets preaching, praying, and doing penance.

The plague subsided, then ceased. An early version of the Black Death eradicated by prayerful singing.

Pope Gregory then turned back to his plainsong work.

HARMONIOUS FACT: The International Red Cross took musicians on a tour of trouble spots on the African continent. The musicians involved hoped to combat the violence and wars across Africa by joining local bands and replacing ethnic discrimination with musical brotherhood. A Kora player at a camp in northern Kenya shared the special meaning that music—especially singing— holds for him. "I was injured when my village in Sudan was attacked one night," he said. "When day broke, I started singing, which attracted the attention of passers-by, who took me here where my leg was amputated." A musician in a refugee land whose leg was lost, but whose life was saved by singing a song.

TEN WAYS TO SING AND SAVE A LIFE

1. Researchers believe that making music, attending cultural events, and singing in groups may cause people to live longer. The heightened emotional states stimulate the immune system to better attack infections. *Sing and extend your life by improving your resistance to disease.*

2. During the aftermath of the first World Trade Center disaster — the bombing — the 50,000 employees escaped the disabled building by tramping down hundreds of flights of stairs in the dark, keeping calm by counting the steps and singing songs. *Sing and save your life by remaining calm.*

3. During the second World Trade Center disaster, a hero named Rick Rescorla in the South Tower saved the lives of many employees and visitors by singing with them as he helped them evacuate the building. *Sing and save lives by keeping others calm.*

4. A popular Civil War song "All Quiet Along the Potomac Tonight," told the story of a guard shot on duty. The singing of the song brought the situation to the attention of the public who protested such actions on both sides and managed a prohibition of sorts against shooting the indefensible and easily killed sentries. *Sing and save lives by making known a deadly situation.*

5. Yoko Ono saved her mother's life by keeping her concious during a serious health attack; she sang and encouraged her mother to sing a song familiar to them both, a song with emotional appeal. When people become mentally disoriented, suffer a physical disruption, or become overwhelmed with anxiety, especially in a life-threatening situation, a song can calm both the victim and the rescuer until professional help arrives. Talk to your loved ones to discover the songs most likely to trigger a strong or calming emotional response for them in a crisis. Jot these titles down and keep a copy handy in a wallet or purse. *Sing and save a loved one's life with a familiar song.*

6. A popular story across the Internet tells how three-year-old Michael wanted to sing for his baby sister. According to the story, she is born with complications, put into intensive care, and may not survive. Michael manages to get into the intensive care unit and sings his song. His baby sister recovers. Church members close to the family say the story is true. Naysayers have set up entire websites to prove it false. Fact or urban legend, we might take a cue from the story and consider singing for the desperately ill or comatose. Our song might reach the still functioning corners of the brain and trigger a response. *Sing and reach out to the nearly dead.*

7. Basketball great Dennis Rodman contemplated suicide with a rifle. He got into his truck and reached out—not for the rifle, but for the sound system. He turned on his favorite group, Pearl Jam. After listening to their songs, he rejected suicide and changed his life. ***Sing and touch a troubled heart.***

8. Arion the bard stood on the bow of the weathered Greek ship, stared at the bearded pirates, and caught sight of the skewered captain being cast overboard portside. The bard and his lyre would be next. To the surprise of the mutineers, the singer broke out in his swan song , then flung himself overboard to avoid their swords. A blue column of smooth marine beast shot between the singer's legs and lifted the sinking man above the choppy waves. A passing dolphin, attracted and enchanted by Arion's song, hoisted the singer upon his back and carried him off towards the mainland. Arion's story is so ancient, it is considered only a legend, but his example is still relevant. ***Sing, and help may come from unknown sources.***

9. Eric Kinworthy sang a song of faith and saved his life. The submarine crew sang a song of faith and saved themselves. Whole books have been devoted to the power of a hymn or religious song in a time of need. ***Sing and be saved by the power of faith.***

10. Singing songs might trigger occasional miracles; knowing lifesaving strategies can produce common miracles. Everyone should be trained in cardiopulmonary resuscitation; the key elements from the training can be condensed and remembered with a song. Here are the ABCs of CPR in verse form to the tune of the original-everybody-knows-the-piano-version "Heart and Soul." ***Sing and remember life-saving procedures.***

David Francis Dayton

The ABCs of CPR

(Sung to the tune of "Heart and Soul")

You can learn—no matter where you are,
The ABCs —of giving CPR.
You can learn —to save a life today
So listen to what I say.

Open the airway—with a head/chin lift.
Clear the mouth—and give two breaths to start.
Check the neck—to see if there's a pulse.
If none, do four cycles of chest compression.

Continue until—the person's breathing again
On his own—or till some help arrives.
Adapt them—for an infant or a child.
A child requires adaptation.

David Francis Dayton

Sing Out and You May Save a Life

(Sung to the tune of "Impossible Dream")

Sing out and you may save a life.
Sing out and you may save your wife.
Sing out and you may save your husband.
Sing out and you may save your child.

Sing out when you walk in a coal miner's cave!
Sing out when you're sunk in a watery grave.
Sing out when the doc says there isn't a chance.
Sing out and you may see the dolphins come dance.

Sing out for a king.
Sing out under a knife.
Sing out for yourself
And you may save your life.
Yes, you may save your life.
And the world will be stunned when you do.
But the world will have nary a clue.
When it sees how you handle your strife
When you sing, yes you sing for your life.

IV.
SING AND FIND SUCCESS

The Man Who Sang Himself Into Chairman of the Board

In *How to Succeed in Business Without Really Trying*, a window washer reads a book and sings the rules for business success. Suddenly he is hired into the mailroom. Through a series of songs and stage twists, he rises to the position of Vice President of Advertising.

But the ax is about to fall.

A failed television ad campaign, plus an attack upon the building by mad treasure hunters, plus an outraged chairman of the board combine to threaten the success of the once-upon-a-time window washer.

Then he sings one more song, "Brotherhood of Man."

David Francis Dayton

One song unravels the company's troubles, patches up all problems between management and labor, and raises the window washer another level on the ladder of success.

Singing makes him Chairman of the Board.

Can singing grant you greater success in life?

Here are Mark Twain, Julie Andrews, and Elvis Presley to prove that it can. But first, some musings about successful singing by Broadway legend Robert Goulet...

MAY 19, 2000

DEAR DAVID,

I SING BECAUSE I CAN!

I ENJOY SINGING AND I TRY TO KEEP MY BODY IN SHAPE SO THAT I MAY PRODUCE THE SOUNDS THAT I LIKE TO MAKE. BEYOND THAT, IS INTERPRETATION!

SO MANY POP AND ROCK ARTISTS SING NOISE — NO NEED FOR THOUGHT OR FOR REACHING ANY SORT OF DEPTH OF UNDERSTANDING IN RELATION TO THE LYRICS. (WELL, FIRST YOU NEED GOOD LYRICS.)

I ...HOPE MY FEW SENTENCES CAN BE OF SOME HELP TO YOU—

ROBERT GOULET

20. The Singing Abolitionist (c. 1850)

She gave him the gift of sweet song.
—Homer

Have you heard of the singing abolitionist?

John Greenleaf Whittier wrote a song and taught folks to sing it to encourage free-state emigration to Kansas. If Kansas received enough free-staters, the vote would swing and Kansas would enter the Union as a Free State. Abolitionist John Greenleaf Whittier failed.

However, abolitionist Harriet Tubman succeeded. At seven, she made her own first escape from slavery, and only returned when she ran out of food. At thirteen, she tried to save another slave from severe punishment and received a two-pound weight to the head which cracked her skull. Years afterwards, she lived with periodic blackouts. Harriet left her husband behind and escaped slavery at last, running up the Underground Railroad to Philadelphia.

Once free, she turned right around and laid plans to free others. The Congress passed the Fugitive Slave Act and made it illegal to help a runaway slave. Man's laws mattered little to Harriet. She slipped into Maryland and returned with her sister and her sister's children.

She never lost an underground passenger, and brought back three hundred slaves into the golden glory of freedom in just eighteen trips. On her nineteenth trip, she rescued her parents.Stung by her success, the South put forty thousand dollars out for her capture. No one ever collected the reward.

What made Harriet such an expert railroader? Many things.

First, her seriousness of purpose. She carried a gun—not for protection against Southerners, but to discourage the runaways from quitting in midflight. When the Civil War began, she quickly joined the Union army and set off on military campaigns. During one campaign alone, she saved 750 slaves.

Second, her brilliant genius for instant strategy. When one hostile party got close on her heels, she directed her group to catch a train running due South. The hostile party never expected runaways to head South. The slaves later jumped the train and headed north once again.

Third, her sweet voice. Harriet often sang her charges out of trouble.

The cold moon shines on Maryland trees in 1850. Hounds bay in the distance as a barefoot man in rags stops on the damp ground by an oak, breathing hard. Should he run into the forest? The hounds would run him down. Should he scramble up the oak? The trackers would finish him with a rifle shot. Then comes a song.

Wade in the water....wade in the water, children, now!

The voice of an underground railroad leader comes singing into the slave's ears. Smiling, the fugitive breaks for a stream and strides across ankle-deep. Water flies from his toes as he slips into the forest on the far side and disappears into a warm summer night.

The hounds hold up at the water and lose the trail. By the time the riflemen arrive, the trail is cold, the bloodhounds are confused, and the once hopeless man is headed for freedom. Another slave saved by the singing of a tuned-in abolitionist. Another slave set free by the crucial directive hidden in a song.

HARMONIOUS FACT: Former slaves have testified that the songs sung in bondage represented an essential means by which they communicated among themselves, fought back against their oppressors, and reclaimed the power of self-definition.

---

21. What's in a Name? (c. 1850)

*It sank deep into his heart, like the melody of a song
sounding from out of childhood's days.*
—Jean Paul Richter

Mark Twain is considered the best humorist in American literature. His books and tales have pleased both children and adults. If you have not read *The Adventures of Huckleberry Finn, The Adventures of Tom Sawyer, The Prince and the Pauper*, or *A Connecticut Yankee in King Arthur's Court*, then as sure as there is mud in the Mississippi, you have probably seen a stage or film production based on one of his works. His name evokes a white-suited gentleman with cotton-candy hair and combed cotton mustache, clutching a cigar and reminiscing about "life on the Mississippi."

Some scholars will tell you Twain's newspaper career gave him the critical push into the public arena. (It does help to have a brother who runs a printing press.)

Some scholars will tell you that a tale told in a miner's camp about a fixed frog contest in Calavaras gave Twain the story straw he needed to spin out literary gold. (A funny yarn from the West sure made Lincoln's death and those Civil War blues easier to cope with.)

Some scholars will tell you almost anything about Mr. Twain. Their courage in proposing outlandish theories has given me the courage to tell you the truth. Mark Twain's entire literary career rocketed to success...because of a song.

Before I prove it, hold on to your jumping amphibians, and let me introduce you to the flip side of Missouri's literary coin—Thomas Jefferson Snodgrass.

Thomas Jefferson Snodgrass was no relation to the Presidential writer of the Declaration of Independence, but he was a writer. His name evokes no images, but his works are as well-known as Mark Twain's. He wrote in the same vein, the same historic period, and with the same palette of regional color. None but the historian knows him, but nearly the whole world is familiar with his literary output.

Like Twain, Snodgrass grew up in Missouri and once

piloted steamboats up and down the Mississippi.

Like Twain, Snodgrass once heroically joined the Confederate army, then quietly ran off when the glory of the enterprise faded.

Like Twain, Snodgrass once owned a silver mine worth a million dollars, but neglected to officially stake the claim and lost it.

At the height of the Cold War, Russia considered Thomas Jefferson Snodgrass to be America's greatest author. Oxford University granted Thomas Jefferson Snodgrass an honorary degree for his accomplishments in literature.

In his time, Snodgrass was so well-known and so appreciated, he could travel to any country in the civilized world, give a talk or read from one of his many popular "funny" books, and reap a fortune.

But Thomas Jefferson Snodgrass did not begin with golden letters. He began with broad, biting satire—the kind that made enemies and varnished his reputation as a crude frontier newsman. The wild style made some quick money, but Snodgrass found himself limited by the pseudonym he chose to write under. He needed another pen name—one that would allow him to be satirical like Thomas Jefferson Snodgrass, but also warm, humorous, reflective, nostalgic— whatever he chose. He needed a name that would not stereotype him. A name that would be appropriate to his life. A name that would go down in history as the "Lincoln of our Literature."

Snodgrass found his perfect name in a song. He recalled his life on the Mississippi and the chant the riverboat men used to sing out when the water was deep enough for a steamboat to plunge safely through. He lifted the full chant, christened it his byline, and sailed safely ahead into success.

For Thomas Jefferson Snodgrass was but one of the many aliases of Samuel Langhorne Clemens. Sam tried out dozens before he found the pen name which resulted in a pot of gold from Virginia City to San Francisco to New York.

Yes, Clemen's career bogged down as bad as buckshotted frog Dan'l Webster...until he changed his name to the short riverboat chant "two fathoms by the mark".

Or, as the riverboat men used to sing out,

"Mark Twain!"

HARMONIOUS FACT: When Miss Kapplehoff auditioned as a singer for bandleader Barney Rapp, he suggested she use a stage name. She immediately selected "Day" from her tryout song, "Day After Day," and went on to fame and fortune as Doris Day.

---

22. The Cowboy's Secret Weapon (c.1880)

In whose heart there is no song, to him the miles are many and long.
—Anonymous

Mamas, don't let your sons grow up to be cowboys. Fingers caught between the rope and the saddle might soon be missed. One bad fall from a spooked mustang could break a leg. A kick from the same horse could mean death. Far from town, cowboys doctored themselves and buried their buddies.

And what about those "cows?" Cowboys had to tug cattle from quicksand, detach them from barbed wire fences, and pull them from mud. They could shoot horses, but they had to tend injured cattle. And when a cow gave birth, the cowboy turned veterinarian—he had to stand and deliver.

Cowboys embody the frontier spirit of America. A movie cowboy is a masterpiece of courage—fast on the draw, solving problems with his guts and his gun.

In reality, a cowboy rarely carried his gun. Guns proved impractical. A cowboy could not ride with his gun. A cowboy could not afford bullets for his gun. He could put a horse out of its misery or stop a rattlesnake with a point-blank shot. He could ride into town on payday and impress the locals. But a gun was mostly a nuisance. The cowboy relied on a better weapon to battle his worst enemy.

Lightning flashes from the sky, but thunder comes from the earth. This rolling thunder shakes the ground with vibrations strong as an earthquake. A thousand pointed spikes are blasting forth at the heads of half a thousand living locomotives chugging up turf and spitting up dust as they bolt forward in mechanical motion.

The mass of mad animals smashes through all obstacles—tents, wagons, human flesh—snorting hot cattle breathe in men's faces before trampling them underneath and wetting the prairie with their blood. The cowboy's worst enemy, and the thing he feared the most on his cattle drive, was a stampede.

Many great cowboy stories have been handed down about the handling of sudden stampedes.

Henry C. Wall caught a stampede coming full speed in his direction with no rock or tree at hand to hide behind. He seized the horn of one steer, ran by its side for an hour, and succeeded in leading it outside the herd to a safe area for his release.

Another quick-thinking cowboy opened a big bag of salt from his ranch, galloped across the stampeding herd's course and emptied the sack. Every steer sniffed the line of salt and the stampede broke up.

One common method for derailing a stampede was to send a brave horseman out to the front of the herd to take the lead away from the advancing animals. Once the cattle were accustomed to following the lead horse, the rider would begin a circling pattern which would end in the steers milling about until coming to a full stop.

But stampede stopping did not prove popular. Cowboys could not afford playing hero. They were their own doctors. An improperly set broken bone left a cowboy crippled for life. And the circumstances leading to stampede could occur one hundred times on every cattle drive.

So the cowboy doctors went in for stampede prevention, and they relied on one special tool—invented by a cowboy—to keep the cows under control. The cowboys employed the invention most during the dangerous shift from eleven at night until two in the morning when cattle were most likely to get up and stretch and be startled.

See the blue silver desert shining under the moon's pale light while a coyote yaps on the near hills. Stars sparkle in the black sky while the campfire sparks below. The cattle are milling.

A storm threatens far off with yellow dashes of lightning, but it is moving away. The cattle do not know that. The coyote's yaps now explode into long, shaking wails; he is calling to his mate. The cattle do not know that. Cattle travel hundreds of miles through uncanny territory. Not a homey sight anywhere. Any strange sound can ignite the dry timbering herd into a blaze of trampling death.

What can a cowboy do to prevent a stampede? He can break out his special invention—his secret weapon.

Remember the movie cowboy? I lied to you. I led you on, letting you believe (maybe you already believed it) that the movie cowboy gained fame and a following for his gunfighting. He did not. The movie cowboy also relied on the real cowboy's secret weapon to make himself a cinematic success.

Papas don't let your sons grow up to be cowboys. A cowboy's life was plain dull. The cowboy had to deal with the long lonely ride along the trail—hours of rolling with not much to think about, not much to say, and not much to do.

But the cowboy did have one thing to break the monotony and console him in his boredom. And he used that one thing to quiet the cattle and settle them down at night. And that one thing made the first movie cowboys into big stars.

The cowboy's secret weapon was "The Cowboy's Lullaby," a set of verses gently sung to lull the cattle into peace under a black and foreign sky.

Sometimes it worked. Sometimes it did not. But in any case, the real cowboy believed he prevented stampedes and the movie cowboys did find success—by singing a song.

HARMONIOUS FACT: Sailors sang sea songs not only to pass the time, but to do the work; "Whisky Johnnie"—one of the oldest of the halyard shanties—was used for the larger and heavier tasks aboard ship such as hoisting sail and catting the anchor.

---

23. The Captain and His Choir (c. 1937)

When you know the notes to sing, you can sing most anything.
—Oscar Hammerstein II

Money isn't everything. Captain Von Trapp never lacked money. He even hired a governess for his children. The governess then became his wife. Soon the whole family became a happy singing troupe. The Von Trapps would not lack for money. Besides family fortune and family career, the Nazis wanted to give Captain Von Trapp an important post in the German Navy.

Captain Von Trapp refused to work for the Nazis. A good choice, but badly timed. The local officials rushed to his house to arrest the Captain, and "escort" him to his new post.

So goes the version as recorded in Rodgers and Hammerstein's *The Sound of Music.* The movie showed the Von Trapp family sneaking off in the black of night pushing a silent car, hoping to avoid their father's capture.

They are captured nevertheless, but the father has an "ace in the hole." "I can't leave now for the Navy," says Captain Von Trapp. "The Von Trapp Family singers have to compete at a festival." Off go the Von Trapps with a doubting guard.

At the festival, escape seems impossible. Guards at the exits. Guards in the audience. When the performance is over, Papa Von Trapp will be taken to his assigned command as a Nazi captain in the Nazi navy. But Papa Von Trapp has a different plan in mind.

The children dismiss themselves from stage one by one by singing. Taken totally unaware, the Nazis let the family sing their way through their fingers.

Did the real Von Trapps escape from the Nazis in such a daring manner?

No. But they did rely on singing to save the family. The real Von Trapp family saw the threat of war coming and left the country. They financed their escape and survived in America by giving concerts. Agathe, 82, the oldest surviving

Trapp daughter, says singing became the family's key to survival. A series of concerts scheduled in America allowed them to leave Europe in 1938. After going from Austria to Italy, they booked passage to the United States.

"If we hadn't had those concerts in America, we would have been in a bad situation," Agathe says. "It was the providence of God that we were able to sing together."

Sing and find success. On stage and in real life. Even when your obstacles are Nazis.

HARMONIOUS FACT: When the Nazis ordered the Norwegians to close their ancient Trondheim Cathedral, the Norwegians successfully defied the order by singing "A Mighty Fortress Is Our God."

---

24. The Four-Octave Wonder (c. 1939)

*It is the only way to know where Nature hath bestowed
the gift of a good voyce.*
—William Byrd

Working people need entertainment, too. In the nineteenth century, vaudeville and burlesque came into being to meet the needs of the working people with music, dance, comedy and specialty acts.

In England, the term Music Hall stood for the tavern and stage show that proved such an excellent training ground for the stars of the forties and fifties who found television to be an electronic version of the old vaudeville variety show.

Of course, not all music hall entertainers reached the heights of Broadway or Hollywood or the coming medium of television. Some just lived for the acclaim of the small stage, survived and paid the bills. One such woman was Barbara Wells.

Barbara Wells divorced school teacher Ted Wells and joined up with another Ted to form a vaudeville team in 1939. Her big problem after the divorce concerned her four-year-old daughter, Julia Elizabeth Wells. How would Julia get along with a new father?

The solution came with singing. Barbara asked her tenor husband to give singing lessons to daughter Julia. Maybe working together would foster a father-daughter relationship.

Father and daughter sang together so well, Barbara pushed for Julia to join the family act and sent her to singing teacher Lillian Stiles-Allen for advanced lessons. Lillian praised Julia's talent, but expressed reluctance to train the now seven-year-old girl for fear of damaging her young vocal chords.

The parents sent Julia to throat specialists to quash Lillian's concerns and the throat specialists made an amazing discovery. The seven-year-old girl's throat contained a fully developed adult larynx. The physical evidence explained the girl's incredible four-octave range.

Julia Elizabeth Wells sang for British soldiers, for packed music halls, and even for the queen. She won the lead in *My Fair Lady*, but did not get the role for the movie. The producers chose to go with a big name.

So Julia sang in a competing movie and won the Oscar for best actress, handily defeating Audrey Hepburn in *My Fair Lady*. She next sang in the biggest box office smash of all time and received the winning vote for the world's most popular actress.

All this acclaim because Julia's parents used singing to help Julia connect with her stepfather. All this success because a four-year-old sang to build a bridge to her second dad.

The singing worked; Julia even took her second dad's surname. We now call her Julie Andrews—star of *Mary Poppins* and *The Sound of Music*.

Sing and solve your family problems. Sing and be a star.

HARMONIOUS FACT: Parents can increase family bliss by introducing singing throughout the day. Singing in the morning can encourage youngsters to get ready for school. Singing at the grocery store or in the car can help children survive wait time. Singing in the evening can calm down babies enough to sleep.

---

25. The Singing Prisoners (c. 1930s)

If you cannot teach me to fly teach me to sing.
—Sir James Barrie

Research is a tricky thing. Who are you going to believe? The researchers or the man himself?

Huddie tried to escape from prison several times. In his seventh year of a thirty year sentence in Texas, performing hard labor in chain gangs, he was getting tired. His first escape failed and resulted in harsh punishment.

So Huddie resigned himself to getting along with the inmates and the prison personnel as best he could. He became a favorite of the guards for his guitar playing and singing. Then the singing inspired him. He decided to plea for his release by singing on his own behalf.

If I had you, Governor Neff, like you got me

I'd wake up in the morning and set you free.

Maybe the governor already appreciated the prisoner's talents. Maybe the "please pardon me" song really did have an effect. In either case, Huddie or "Walter Boyd" was released from jail in 1925. Governor Patt Neff apparently came through, granting the pardon as he himself left office.

Huddie could not keep himself out of trouble. Once again he found himself in prison. Now he would get help from another source.

A Northern musical historian drove his beat-up Ford across the American South, seeking out singers to record hours of blues, country, and work songs. The music Mr. Lomax collected would later inspire the birth of rock and roll, country, and even rap. On one trip to a prison in Lousiana, Mr. Lomax recorded Huddie, or "Leadbelly" as he became better known, who took advantage of the moment to appeal for another pardon through his song. He also sang his trademark tune, "Goodnight Irene," and addressed his work to Louisiana Governor O. K. Allen. The song made it to the governor and six months later, Leadbelly found freedom once again.

Huddie died in late 1949, with the legacy of a musical giant. His guitar playing and impassioned voice gave life to an array of biographical characters that inhabited his songs. Many of Leadbelly's numerous compositions are classics, such as "Midnight Special" (later recorded by Creedence Clearwater Revival) and "Rock Island Line" (recorded by Johnny Cash). He died penniless, but within six months his song "Goodnight, Irene" became a million-record hit for the singing group, The Weavers, and the rest of his compositions changed the face of music around the world.

Researchers say that none of his songs played any part in his pardons or releases from prison. Leadbelly maintained they did. Believe the researchers and look for another miracle. Else, believe the man himself.

HARMONIOUS FACT: How was social activist Eugene Debs inspired to work for prison reform? While in prison, he heard a convict sing a spiritual. The experience moved him to add prisoners to his list of social concerns.

26. The Secretary Who Sang Herself Into the Movies (c.1929)

Tis a sure sign work goes on merrily, when folks sing at it.
                    —Isaac Bickerstaffe

Frances needed a song break. But Frances could not get a singing job.

Instead, at fourteen, Frances eloped with her childhood sweetheart to Memphis. At fifteen, she gave birth to her first child and her teenage husband left her.

Mama moved to Memphis and Frances moved in with Mama. Now Frances got a job. Not a singing job, but a job that paid the bills and kept her in good relationship with Mama. She worked in an insurance office.

Insurance or not, Frances still wanted to sing. She carried grand ideas in her head about becoming a singer and building a singing career. And even though this didn't seem to be the place to make such dreams come true, Francis sang anyway—right there in the office, right there among the file cabinets.

Then her boss came in and caught her singing on the job. He removed her from the office at once....and put her on the radio on Friday nights, at a radio station he happened to own. Frances began her singing career.

She sang and played piano on a series of radio programs as Frances Fox. Then she changed her name to Marian Lee, hoping for more success. Finally a station manager changed her name for her. He took an actress from the silent film era and hooked on a euphonious surname. Frances Fox—Marian Lee—now became Dale Evans.

Dale Evans sang her way to Chicago where she joined a number of big bands and soloed in notable hotels such as the Blackstone, the Sherman, the Drake, and the Chez Paree Supper Club. Talent scouts from Paramount picked her up for a screen test in Hollywood, but her weak dancing (not her singing) kept her from a part in *Holiday Inn* with Fred Astaire and Bing Crosby.

Dale kept singing until Republic Studios signed her on to star in several movies, including a John Wayne western. Then came her biggest break and biggest role when Herbert Yates put her into *The Cowboy and the Senōrita,* matching her with Roy Rogers.

Her success led to a television series with Roy and singing appearances throughout the world. Dale's personal honors include The Texas Press Association's Texan of the Year (1970); Cowgirl Hall of Fame (1995); Cardinal Terrence Cook Humanities Award (1995); and three stars on The Hollywood Walk of Fame.

All this from singing....on the job.

HARMONIOUS FACT: How did Roy Rogers land his motion-picture contract? He sang "The Last Roundup."

27. Baby, Take a Bow (c. 1934)

A persuasive thing is song; let girls learn to sing.
—Ovid

President George Bush appointed her ambassador to Czechoslovakia in 1989. Before that, she served as U.S. ambassador to Ghana from 1974 until 1976, when she became U.S. chief of protocol. Before that, in 1968, President Nixon appointed her ambassador to the United Nations.

Thirty years before that, in 1938, she topped all other Hollywood stars as the number one box-office attraction in America. Cute, dimpled, precocious, and doll-like, she provided a "Curly Top" diversion during the Depression years of the 1930s. At the height of her success she was an institution—a model daughter for every mother, a model child for every little girl to imitate. A whole industry developed around a single star and her phenomenal success: dolls, coloring books, dresses, everything. No child star had ever before been so popular with the public.

None has since.

Born on April 23, 1928 in Santa Monica, California, Shirley Temple began life as the daughter of a bank teller. She took dancing classes at three and appeared in a series of one-reel films before she reached the age of four. The series, called *Baby Burlesks* (1931), consisted of take-offs on popular movies of the time, with Shirley playing the leading lady roles, imitating Marlene Dietrich and other famous stars.

One-reel films did not make Shirley a phenomenal star. She had to sing first. Here is one version of the legend.

A three-year-old girl, waiting in the background of a 20th Century Fox movie set, started dancing about to keep amused. A director noticed her steps and in a burst of inspiration decided to try something. He hurriedly scribbled the words of a popular song "Baby, Take a Bow" on the back of an envelope and asked her to learn the words at once. She did. She went on to perform the song for an astonished collection of actors, cameramen, crew and cast who gave her instant recognition by falling into complete silence after her performance.

"By God," thundered Harold Lloyd, breaking the silence, "here's another Jackie Coogan." Executives immediately signed her to a contract and gave her a starring role in *Stand Up and Cheer*, catapulting the name ShirleyTemple into child-star fame. At the end of her first year as a child star, she received a special Academy Award "in grateful recognition of her outstanding contribution to screen entertainment during the year 1934."

From one-reelers to an Oscar, thanks to a song.

Doubt the power of her singing?

In the same year of her first film, Shirley sang "On the Good Ship Lollipop" and sold more than 400,000 copies in sheet music form. She outsold the best singers of the time, including the great Bing Crosby. Singing made a little girl into an institution. Singing made a little girl into a success.

HARMONIOUS FACT: Three-year-olds who received twice weekly singing lessons showed greater improvement than a control group on measures of motor development, abstract conceptual thinking, play improvisation, originality, and verbal abilities.

---

28. The Throw-Away Hit (c. 1942)

*It is the best of all trades to make songs
and the second best to sing them.*
—Hilaire Belloc

How to Succeed In Business Without Really Trying received the Pulitzer Prize in 1962. *Guys and Dolls* received two Tony awards and made it to the motion picture arena with Frank Sinatra and Marlon Brando. *Most Happy Fella* and *Where's Charley?* both continue to be happily revived.

Add in the score for *Hans Christian Andersen*, the academy award-winning song, "Baby, It's Cold Outside," 1948's leading hit, "On a Slow Boat to China," and the official song of the Infantry, "What Do You Do in the Infantry?" and you will have a slight idea of what the world would have missed if Frank Loesser had not been singing on a particular day in a particular way.

Despite his piano-teacher father's efforts to the contrary, Loesser dropped out of the City College of New York to became a music publisher's staff lyricist in the late 1920s. In 1936 he moved to Hollywood and became an accomplished lyricist, collaborating with Hoagy Carmichael on "Small Fry" and "Two Sleepy People" and with Joseph J. Lilley on "Jingle, Jangle, Jingle." Other composers for whom he wrote lyrics included Burton Lane, Jule Styne, Arthur Schwartz, Frederick Hollander, and Jimmy McHugh.

Please note: Frank Loesser is the lyricist. This means that all the plays and hits listed above might have been ours in words only. Frank never contemplated writing music to his words until one incidental day during World War II.

On that day, Frank Loesser tested out his words again to the same throw-away tune he used for most of his songwriting tasks. He always wrote the words and then handed them on to someone else to add the music. To better work the words, he often made up a quick tune in his head to patter out the rhythm and rhyme of his verses.

This song would become the number one hit of World War II. When the Japanese bombed Pearl Harbor, a Navy chaplain cried out, "Praise the Lord and pass the ammunition!" Frank seized on the quote as a seed for a moving, timely song, a patriotic salute to America's entry into the war.

Once Frank finished the words, he sang his war hit for several friends using the old tune as "window dressing" to the words. Not only did his friends agree to the words, they insisted he use the tune as well. Frank's military theme, "Praise the Lord and Pass the Ammunition," sold over two million copies in 1942 and received so much airplay that the government had to restrict its time on the radio to avoid excessive exposure.

Most importantly, singing "Praise" changed Frank's whole way of doing things. Now he felt capable of writing the music as well as the words. Thanks to singing one song to his friends, Mr. Loesser went on to write both words and music, giving the musical theater such enduring works as "Guys and Dolls," "How to Succeed In Business Without Really Trying," and "Most Happy Fella."

Think of what we would have missed if Frank had not been singing his own song that fateful day.

HARMONIOUS FACT: In 1920, the manager of the Primrose & West Company planned to fire Eddie Leonard, so he told the singer-composer to go ahead and sing whatever he wanted for his final performance with the minstrel troupe. Eddie saved his job by composing and singing his own smash hit, "Ida! Sweet as Apple Cider."

---

29. The Sound of Success (c. 1960s)

Those who wish to sing always find a song.
—Swedish Proverb

It happens all the time on Broadway. It happens all the time in the movies. But this time it happened in real life—to musical writer extraordinaire, Stephen Sondheim. Stephen Sondheim's first attempt to marry words to music almost ended in divorce. The reviews of the show skewered the cast, director, and writer.

One critic warned them they were getting very near "amateur night."

The main reviewer simply suggested, "Close the show."

Down $100,000 and ready to give up, Sondheim sat in a motel room in Washington and reexamined his situation. Who else could claim the theatre background he grew up with? Oscar Hammerstein II tutored him in theatre arts as a child. At 17, Sondheim helped produce Rogers and Hammerstein shows.

Curtains opened as Sondheim composed and created. He wrote music for television. He debuted on Broadway as a lyricist, teaming up with the talents of Leonard Bernstein and Jule Styne. His early collaborations gave us the ground-breaking *West Side Story* and the Broadway classic *Gypsy*.

Now Sondheim felt ready to do it all. No more music alone. No more lyrics for someone else's tunes.

Sondheim wrote the entire package for what should have been a successful farce. But the only thing funny about *A Funny Thing Happened on the Way to the Forum* was the funny way the audience reacted to the show. They did not realize what they were watching—they did not understand they were supposed to be laughing.

No farce triumphs if no one laughs. The producer knew it. The director knew it. The actors knew it. And Stephen Sondheim, sitting in his hotel room alone, knew it worst of all.

The crew called down Jerry Robbins who originally planned to direct the show and he saw the problem at once. He made some staging changes, but the biggest change was sending Sondheim out to write a fresh opening number for the show's clowns.

Someday, someone as talented as Sondheim will write a musical based on that electrifying day. It was pure theatre. Sondheim locked himself in a room with a piano and set about saving his musical. All he needed to do was write a perfect showstopping song.

He wrote the song.

The musical opened in New York. The musical became a smash. As Sondheim later put it, the new song "not only brought down the house, but the entire show was clearly a hit...and it was all a matter of the opening number."

It happens all the time on Broadway. It happens all the time in the movies. But this time it happened in real life.

Stephen Sondheim's first attempt at writing both words and music for a show was a looming disaster until he saved the show by writing just one more song—"Comedy Tonight."

HARMONIOUS FACT: The star, the producer, the director, and the cast united in their verdict that the cowboy western they had just completed would be just that—a "cowboy western" and nothing more. But movie composer Dmitri Tiomkin had another idea; he wrote "Do Not Forsake Me," a song that encapsulated the story plot and pushed the film into hit status. Frankie Laine's recording of the theme went gold and had much to do with turning *High Noon* into a 1952 Oscar-winning classic instead of a forgotten cowboy flick.

30. A Record for Mama (c. 1953)

None sing so wildly well as the angel Israfel.
—Edgar Allen Poe

1953 looked like the end of an era.

Joseph Stalin died. Konrad Adenauer, Chancellor of the West German Republic, won Man of the Year. The United States returned the captured northern Ryukyu Islands to Japan. World War II became fixed in the past. The Korean War ended and the Cold War between democracy and communism began.

Nature magazine published the double helix structure of the DNA molecule, setting the stage for the biotechnology revolution.

With space thrillers *Invaders From Mars* and *War of the Worlds* fresh in the public's mind, and a rash of UFO sightings across the nation, the average American might have guessed that the next upheaval in society would come from something speeding through the sky.

It did not. It came from a four-wheeled vehicle rolling around Memphis, Tennessee.

On Saturday afternoon on one of the final days of 1953's summer, a truck driver for Crown Electric stopped in town on his lunch break to put together a small gift for his mother.

Most other truck drivers might stop at a flower store. Most other truck drivers might put together a box of candy. But this truck driver had a plan for a unique gift. He pulled up in front of a recording studio.

The Memphis Recording Service operator set up the equipment, took the money, and cued the truck driver when to come in. He covered two Ink Spots ballads, "My Happiness" and "That's When Your Heartaches Begin."

Two songs recorded for Mama. One thin black plastic disk instead of a bouquet of flowers or a box of candy. But Mama loved to hear her boy sing. That is why she bought him a guitar. She would love these songs.

The truck driver drove off with his gift, and left behind the tapes of his work. Sun president Sam Phillips heard those tapes and signed the truck driver to a recording contract with Sun Records. The truck driver, briefly out of the Precision Tool Company, and just out of high school, went on to his career in the charts as Elvis Presley.

Sing a song to please your mother.

Sing a song and find success.

Sing a song and change the world.

HARMONIOUS FACT: Eddie Cochran sang, "Twenty Flight Rock," which brought Paul McCartney and John Lennon together. Tony Sheridan sang, "My Bonnie," which brought Brian Epstein and the Beatles together. The Beatles sang and brought the baby boomers of the world together.

TEN WAYS TO SING AND FIND SUCCESS

1. Black Coffee Sound Productions mixed business experience with a love for music to develop a challenging development program for senior executives. Participants improve in such areas as resonance, communication and stress management. *Sing and improve your potential for executive management.*

2. Teachers already know the power of singing to teach everything from the ABC's to tying shoes. Put your directions for trainees into a simple song (piggyback the lyrics onto a familiar tune) and your trainees will learn procedures faster and remember them longer. *Sing and better train your coworkers.*

3. A better presentation at work is within your grasp if you hum before giving your speech. Voice box muscles perform better when loosened and lubricated by a little pre-presentation singing. *Sing and give a better-sounding presentation.*

4. For thousands of years, manual laborers have sung on the job, believing the songs made the work go better. One thing is for certain, singing alleviates the boredom of servile labor. *Sing and make the work go easier.*

5. Opera and movie star Nelson Eddy sang as a reporter, got fired, then met his vocal coach who was seeking out the "singing reporter." Will Rogers discovered Gene Autry who was strumming a guitar and singing on the job in a telegraph office. Carmen Miranda

worked in a store, sang on the job, and ended up on the radio and thence in the movies. ***Sing on the job and get discovered.***

6. Peddlers used to stand on the street and sing about their products. Today, advertisers concoct jingles for their clients and the world sings about their products. Want to sell your merchandise more effectively? Put it into a song. ***Sing and sell your product.***

7. Need a way to make your interview stand out from the others? A teacher applying for Teacher of the Year took his guitar in with him and sang a culminating song about his merits. He took the nomination and won the award. ***Sing and win the interview.***

8. Looking for a way to pass that college class? Turn the information into lyrics for your favorite song. Learn the material by singing the facts and concepts within the context of the song. ***Sing and acquire the knowledge.***

9. Tactfully look for opportunities to include singing in your work. Can you sing for a customer? Can you sing for a coworker? Can you include a song in a special presentation? These moments will make you memorable. Success follows those who stand out from the rest. ***Sing and be unique.***

10. It's Monday again! Need to beat the blues before you get to work and the blues beat you? Try singing on the way to work. Choose your songs carefully and you'll change your attitude. With a song in your heart and a smile on your face, that promotion could be just around the corner. ***Sing and be a better employee.***

David Francis Dayton

Sing to Change Work
(Sung to: "Polly Wolly Doodle")

Sing a tribute to those you work with.
Sing and change your work environment.
Sing to make your work go easier.
Sing and change your work environment.
Hum before, hum before, hum before you stand and speak.
Sing your presentation well and folks will say you are unique.

Sing to beat the "Monday blues".
Sing and change your work environment.
Sing to calm a customer.
Sing and change your work environment.
Hum before, hum before, hum before you stand and speak.
Sing your presentation well and folks will say you are unique.

V.

SING AND PROMOTE HEALING

The Singing Hospital

In *Musical Doctor*, a film short from 1932, Rudy Vallee heads up a unique hospital. In it, the patients are treated with prescriptions of music and doses of singing.

As men lie groaning and suffering on their beds, the original Betty Boop girl, Mae Questel, moves about them, singing to each one to stop pain.

In another display of the hospital's forte, Dr. Rudy meets with a man in the emergency room. He engages him in brief conversation, but solves the gentleman's painful complaint by coaxing the victim to sing a duet.

Singing can distract us from our physical ailments.

Singing can stop our pain.

Singing can promote our healing.

Here are King David of Israel, Queen Lili'uokalani of Hawaii, and Princess Di to show us singing's power to heal in the most extreme circumstances. But first a word about surviving a blood test, from my daughter, Catherine Dayton.

David Francis Dayton

86

DEAR DAD,

I SANG A SONG TO RELIEVE PAIN WHEN I WAS GETTING MY BLOOD TAKEN. I SANG A SONG NOT TO FEEL THE PAIN AND TO IGNORE THE BLOOD BEING TAKEN BECAUSE THE NURSE WAS SEARCHING THROUGH MY SKIN TO FIND THE VEIN. I WAS HUMMING WITH YOU WHILE I LOOKED AT THE STICKERS THAT I GOT. I TRIED NOT TO NOTICE THE BLOOD BEING TAKEN. AFTER THE BLOOD WAS TAKEN, MOM TOLD ME THAT THEY WERE TRYING TO LOOK FOR THE VEIN WITH THE NEEDLE BECAUSE THEY COULDN'T FIND IT.

I FEEL BETTER THAT I SANG BECAUSE I DIDN'T LOOK AT IT. I SANG BECAUSE IT FELT BETTER WHEN I DIDN'T LOOK AT IT.

SINGING HELPED ME NOT BE AFRAID OF THE NEEDLE, BUT IT DID HURT A LITTLE.

FROM YOUR DAUGHTER.

Catherine Rayton

31. Demons in the Head (c. 1020 B.C.)

He who sings, prays twice.
—St. Augustine

Alone in his chambers, the king felt a blackness crawl over him. Something supernatural—and evil.

"Guards!" screamed the monarch.

The guards arrived, but what use were their weapons against an enemy attacking their king from the inside—savaging his mind and soul?

"An evil spirit is torturing you!" cried the helpless servants. "Order it and we will look for a man skilled in playing the harp. When the demon comes over you, he will play and you will feel better."

The king shrieked again. Then he fell to the cedar floor and breathed an anxious command, "Go then, and find me a skillful harpist and bring him to me!"

The servants left and found a boy of Bethlehem to be a skillful harpist. And so David, son of Jesse, came to the palace and played and sang songs for the king.

The evil spirit left Saul.

The king found comfort in a shepherd's song.

HARMONIOUS FACT: King David introduced a singing form of worship to accompany the ritual sacrifices; he organized the priestly Levites to play music and lead the people in freshly-composed songs of praise, adding to the temple prayers.

---

32. The Swedish Nightingale (c.1840)

She will sing the savageness out of a bear.
—William Shakespeare

Jenny Lind, Swedish singing sensation of the 19th century, made grown men wilt with her remarkable voice. Hans Christian Andersen proposed marriage. She turned him down. American bigwigs in Congress, including the famous Daniel Webster, fell under her spell. The opera and stage star so impressed P. T. Barnum that he undertook to manage her American debut tour. Between Jenny's flexible coloratura and his colorful bombast, they made millions. After all these conquests, Jenny Lind settled down with her pianist and made only request performances.

One request performance took her to London to sing before the Queen.

It should have been a simple court concert.

It would have been a simple court concert.

But another singer had also been invited.

Giulia Grisi—Italy's answer to Sweden's Jenny Lind— also appeared on stage. Giulia Grisi, the "singing flower of beauty," sang in London every season after her debut in 1834. She knew her audience and knew how to "knock 'em dead." But this would be the first time she and Jenny Lind ever appeared together on the same stage and took turns entertaining the same audience.

Two world-class singers on stage together in a duel before the Queen. Circulation in the London press played up the possibilities. Who would win?

The concept of competition never entered Jenny Lind's mind at the time.

But some of it must have been in Giulia Grisi's.

When Jenny walked out to center stage to sing first, she cringed to see Grisi shooting scornful looks across the stage. Disturbed by vicious competition, Jenny almost caved in and quit singing.

Then, inspiration struck.

Jenny concluded her first song. The accompanist struck his final chords. Then, unexpectedly, she asked the pianist to rise and took the vacated seat at the piano herself.

The audience stirred in surprise. Even Grisi must have lowered her scowl from poisonous to puzzlement.

Jenny ran her fingers over the keys in an unpretentious prelude. She called up a song from her youth, an unaffected prayer song she had loved as a child. She had not sung it in years, but now this moment on the stage seemed right for a child's devotional.

She sang out the prayer song and the presence of weighty royalty and scowling competitors faded. Instead, her mind and heart flew back to Sweden and her home and singing at the pianoforte for friends and family.

The plaintive notes floated softly at first. Then the singer threw her whole soul into the prayer. The song ended. Silence.

Jenny lifted her eyes from the piano and looked across the stage once again at the scornful face that had so disconcerted her.

No fierce expression anymore.

Instead, a tear fell from the Italian opera star's eye and Giulia Grisi rushed across the stage to give Jenny an unabashed hug and kiss before the entire London audience and the royal family.

Publicity and public hunger for battle had scarred the singers only momentarily. Love of singing healed and reconciled them again.

HARMONIOUS FACT: Women who sing together develop confidence and experience personal growth; women silenced by abuse who sing together release some of the pain and regain their voices and their ability to speak out.

---

33. A Queen and a Princess (c. 1898)

Just an old sweet song keeps Georgia on my mind.
—Ray Charles

"Aloha 'Oe" is a song of Hawaii. It is a sad song of re-membrance.

Farewell to thee, farewell to thee,

Thou charming one who dwells among the bowers.

One fond embrace before I now depart

Until we meet again.

Perhaps vacationers hear the dying notes of "Aloha 'Oe" as they board the plane back to the mainland. Perhaps native Hawaiians, integrated into the mainland culture, hear the song and remember the island of their birth. But the song was not written for vacationers or nostalgic Hawaiians. The song was written to heal grief.

The last queen of the Hawaiian Islands—Lili'uokalani— ruled from 1891 to 1895. She learned to dress and speak and behave in the ways of polite American society. She learned several languages, and composed music.

Only her music would help the queen retain Hawaii.

She once wrote, "to compose was as natural to me as to breathe. This gift remains a source of the greatest consolation." Queen Lili'uokalani recorded her innermost feelings through song. Her total output numbered one hundred sixty-five pieces. One would become Hawaii's most famous and most important song.

When Lili'uokalani was born in 1838, in Honolulu, many of the old ways had already vanished. Congregationalist missionaries from New England had converted one-third of the Hawaiians to Christianity, banned nudity, and outlawed the hula. The missionaries had developed a written Hawaiian language and taught the entire adult population to read and write. The grandchildren of the missionaries would later overthrow the queen.

Lili'uokalani ascended to the throne on January 29, 1891,

and spent much of her time setting up charitable organizations devoted to public education, health and welfare. She
toured the kingdom and began a campaign to renew her
people.

Her people faced a crisis. The Hawaiians were dying.

From 800,000 in 1778, when westerners first arrived,
they had dwindled to 160,000 a mere fifty years later, slaughtered by epidemics and alcoholism. Hawaiian life vanished
with the Hawaiians. Control of property slipped into minor-
ity missionary hands. Common people soon ended up with
less than one percent of the land.

At Queen Lili'uokalani's coronation, the Hawaiians numbered 40,000, and the treasury announced bankruptcy. The
queen attempted economic reforms and cut her own salary.

Then the U.S. government revoked Hawaii's favored
position on the American sugar market. Hawaiian sugar
growers panicked. The single path to survival would be to
become part of the United States. The missionary grandchildren plotted in secret to unite Hawaii to the U.S.

Annexation was anathema to the queen. She wanted
sovereignty. She further wanted to do away with the forced
constitution contrived by the missionary descendants to
extend their power.

On the morning of January 14, 1893, the queen met with
her cabinet and discussed a new constitution which would
restore to her the powers of a monarch and reestablish the
voting rights of her people. But two of her ministers betrayed
her to the annexationists. Her plans were not accepted.

The business community collected and plotted to overthrow
the monarchy. They drafted papers to establish a new government
and named Judge Sanford Dole to be their president. The American minister, John L. Stevens, in league with the missionary
boys, sent word to an American warship to land a company
of Marines.

By evening, the U.S. Marines took up positions facing
'Iolani Palace and the queen. The following day, the missionary boys proclaimed their Hawaiian government. Within

hours, on behalf of the United States, Stevens recognized the regime. The leaders ordered the queen to resign.

Queen Lili' uokalani kept her own people from rising up. She wanted no Hawaiian blood shed, and believed that the government of the United States would reinstate her despite the opposition of the business community.

But Queen Lili'uokalani suffered house arrest in 'Iolani Palace for eight months, after which she abdicated in return for the release of her jailed supporters. In 1898, the United States formally annexed the Hawaiian Islands. Hawaii was lost.

In that same year, Queen Lili'uokalani composed "Aloha 'Oe" —the lament of two separating lovers—as a farewell to her country.

She sang to grieve her lost Hawaii.

She sang to grieve her lost heritage.

She sang to heal her loss.

HARMONIOUS FACT: In 1997, Elton John sang a new version of his old hit, "Candle in the Wind," to help his country recover from, and the world grieve, the loss of Princess Diana. Money from the sale of the recording supported many of Diana's favorite charities.

---

34. Hearts in San Francisco (c. 1906)

There's a little ditty they're singing in the city.
—Lionel Bart

Singers have been attracted to San Francisco over the years. You might remember Tony Bennett's great hit, "I Left My Heart in San Francisco." You might recall the plethora of songs generated during the sixties when San Francisco became the base of operations for the hippies and the Love Generation.

San Francisco has a history of songs.

Good thing, too.

San Francisco also has a history of natural disasters. On April 18th, 1906, San Francisco suffered one of the worst disasters in United States history.

The violent circling winds of a powerful tornado can exceed three hundred miles per hour. It can destroy almost everything in its path, lifting cattle, automobiles, and even mobile homes into the air. A flood can cause millions in damage and leave millions homeless. But a severe earthquake may release ten thousand times the energy of the first atomic bomb.

An earthquake hit San Francisco in 1906.

Gas mains exploded. Stoves and gas lamps overturned. Electric wires snapped. Fires broke out in numerous sections of the city, and firefighters became ineffective because the city's water mains suffered damage. The people watched helplessly as the fire raged for three days. The firefighters dynamited entire blocks of buildings to stop the spreading flames.

Three thousand people died in the disaster. Two hundred fifty thousand lost their homes. Most of the city lay in ruins. Property damage exceeded 500 million dollars.

But the people of San Francisco rebuilt their city. Within nine years, they hosted the Panama-Pacific International Exposition to honor the opening of the Panama Canal.

How did the San Franciscans manage to rebuild with such enthusiasm and vigor?

They sang.

The San Franciscans appropriated a popular song of the time to support their morale as they dug into the ashes and raised up the Phoenix-like metropolis. "Wait Till the Sun Shines, Nellie" became "Wait Till the Sun Shines, Frisco," as San Franciscans rallied to heal their hearts and reclaim the city to the tune of a popular song.

HARMONIOUS FACT: Tony Bennett's San Francisco hit meant more than just higher record sales. Before the chart topper, he admitted in an interview, "Rock and roll all but ruined me. It seemed that any singer over twenty-five who couldn't play a steel guitar was in trouble." Then he had a date at the Fairmont Hotel in San Francisco, debuted the song, and sang his way back to success.

---

35. The Woman of Silence (c. 1960s)

It is a singular and good remedie
for a stutting and stamering in the speech.
—William Byrd

Movies play in dark, silent rooms. Patrons are expected to be quiet. When the soundtrack begins, the power of the modern sound system drowns out all conversation anyway. But the music of movies is not always loud and brassy. Sometimes the atmosphere of film is penetrated by a poignant song.

Carly Simon has four decades of poignant movie songs to her credit. In 1967, she performed the song, "Long-term Physical Effects," for a work by Milos Forman entitled, *Taking Off*.

In 1977, she recorded "Nobody Does It Better" by Marvin Hamlish for the James Bond hit, *The Spy Who Loved Me*.

In the 1980s, she contributed songs to the John Travolta-Jamie Lee Curtis film *Perfect*, to *Swing Shift* with Goldie Hawn, to *Nothing in Common*, with Tom Hanks. She hit another height with "Coming Around Again" in the movie, *Heartburn*, with Meryl Streep and Jack Nicholson, and capped off the decade with the academy-award-winning "Let the River Run" in *Working Girl*.

In the 1990s Simon released the album, *This Is My Life*, which provided the soundtrack to the Nora Ephron movie of the same title. Of course, the name Carly Simon does not necessarily conjure up a movie. She is better known for her recording success.

Carly began recording songs with "Winkin', Blinkin', and Nod," made with her sister, Lucy, and released under the name, The Simon Sisters. She rose to international stardom with the release of her debut grammy-winning album in 1971, containing her first major hit single, "That's the Way I've Always Heard it Should Be." The song hits, "Anticipation," "No Secrets," and "You're So Vain" took her voice to the limits of the known world.

But once upon a time, Carly Simon's signature voice was silent, silent as the voices in a movie theater—until she was saved by a song. Embarrassment kept Carly Simon's mouth shut. She suffered from a speaking problem so severe that, by the time she entered high school, she had decided to never speak in pubic again. Never again.

The woman who would take pointers from Bob Seeger and Bob Dylan and later sing with James Taylor and Mick Jagger, refused to speak to her high school peers.

What about her singing?

Well, Carly Simon grew up in a musical family. She played classical music and accompanied herself on the uku-lele. She intended at first to be a songwriter, not a singer. But like another well-known stutterer—Mel Tillis—Carly dis-covered that singing and speaking come from different parts of the brain. She who stutters can still sing without staccato.

Salvation for Carly Simon's voice came from her mother. Mrs. Simon found a way for Carly to communicate without betraying her esteem-erasing stutter. Mother employed the advantage of her daughter's talent—using a theory based on Mel Tillis. "If stutterers can eliminate their speech defect while singing," reasoned Mrs. Simon, "why not have Carly sing all the time?"

Mrs. Simon taught Carly to speak rhythmically—in a manner closely related to singing. The method worked both ways. The singing-talk improved her speaking clarity and the talk-singing brought out her voice.

Carly Simon faced other obstacles in her path to sing-ing and songwriting. These obstacles she climbed over, slipped around, or pushed aside. No one can subtract from her personal triumphs in the field of music. But in the field of communication, in breaking the barrier of embarrassment, she received a little help—from her mother, and from the healing techniques of singing a song.

HARMONIOUS FACT: Stroke victims who have lost the ability to speak can sometimes recover their speech by singing. Just as dancing and walking are similar, but use different networks in the brain, the same is true for singing and talking. When one part of the brain is damaged, therapists can look for a detour in some other part. Patients with a stroke on the left, speech-controlling side of the brain can use their singing skills, which are on the right side of the brain, to get their words back, if not by singing, then at least in a sing-song voice.

Nathan Dayton

36. P.O.W.Ȿ (c. 1972)

Tis not in the high stars alone,
Nor in the cups of budding flowers,
Nor in the redbreast's mellow tone,
Nor in the bow that smiles in showers,
But in the mud and scum of things
There alway, alway something sings.
—Emerson

Captain Rutledge bailed out of his dying plane and parachuted down into hostile territory. His F-8 Crusader Jet exploded in flames, and he heard the singing of bullets zipping past his descending body. Finally, he sank several feet deep into rice paddy mud and discovered himself a prisoner of the North Vietnamese.

Cast into a cement-box prison, the officer of captured American forces sat chained and cramped upon a block. Weeks, then months, passed in isolation with no bathroom privileges, scant water, poor food, and little light. The jailers wanted to turn the prisoners into tools of propaganda. Those who would not break would be driven mad. Brainwashed or brain dysfunctional.

Rats and bugs provided company, but no conversation. The captain pushed his mind to work, building houses in his imagination, one board and one nail at a time, and struggled to remember prayers, scriptures, and hymns to console himself.

Other prisoners fared no better. To communicate critical information, the confined men tapped on their doors in Morse code. If they were caught, the Viet Cong guards beat them.

But changes were coming. During the last leg of imprisonment, the prisoners were herded into communal cell blocks where they could meet and converse openly for the first time in years. The first choice for many of them was to pray and praise God with song. They decided to keep it up weekly, choosing various officers to act as chaplains for Sunday services.

The guards did not want the singing or the sermons.

Singing and sermons for the North Vietnamese smelled of political rallies. The makeshift church services were seen as rallying attempts and plotting. The guards interfered, screamed interruptions, and threatened physical abuse.

Captain Rutledge's group refused to give up their services. The next Sunday, they gathered again for the purpose of praising God. The guards hollered and threatened, then angrily marched out of the cell to plan a fitting revenge for the rebellious American soldiers.

Would the prisoners lose the morale they had gained? Would they again be isolated and tortured and reduced to slaves of the enemy—tools of propaganda?

Captain Rutledge and two others most instrumental in the cell-block service were herded out into the courtyard where all the prisoners could witness their particular punishment. The lesson would leave its mark on all the other prisoners—reduce them further down in their humanity.

Then, in Captain Rutledge's own words, "a fantastic thing happened." Somewhere in Cell Block 7, a prisoner began to sing the first verse of "The Star-Spangled Banner." Prohibited on penalty of severe punishment, no one had dared sing it for five years. Now another voice joined in, and another.

O say, can you see, by the dawn's early light,

What so proudly we hailed at the twilight's last gleaming,

By the end of the first line, all of Cell Block 7 had lifted up their voices in a group choir. By the end of the second line, every cell block in the camp had joined in.

O say, does that Star-Spangled Banner yet wave

O'er the land of the free and the home of the brave?

There would be months of imprisonment to endure before Captain Rutledge and most of the compatriots found release and again saw their families, but that moment of song defined their spirit. They would not leave as defeated slaves of the enemy. They would not leave as psychological wrecks abandoned by their homeland through the growing guilt of an "unjust war."

The prisoners had conquered! They found healing through one unifying song.

HARMONIOUS FACT: Outside prison and just after the Civil War, former slaves found work building the huge banks or levees that kept the waters of the Mississippi River from overflowing. From sunup to sundown they hauled dirt with the help of ragged old mules—brutal work under mean taskmasters. To get through the day and give voice against the oppressive conditions, the workers sang "levee hollers" filled with hidden criticism of the bosses.

HARMONIOUS FACT: Following the September 11, 2001, World Trade Center attacks, a group of victims' relatives recorded two songs—"Wake Up Everybody" and "I Cried"—with hip-hop group Angels with Broken Wings. Three-quarters of the proceeds have been pledged to help 9/11 families and contribute to a Ground Zero memorial. Sing and honor the 9/11 heroes.

37. Songs of Love (c. 1996)

To sing is to love and to affirm, to fly and soar, to coast into the hearts of the people who listen, to tell them that life is to live, that love is there, that nothing is a promise, but that beauty exists, and must be hunted for and found.
—Joan Baez

Walking down the street in early 1996, an idea came to singer-songwriter John Beltzer, an idea that would deeply touch many lives. As a way of providing sick children with a source of inspiration, joy and possibly even healing, he set out to create personalized one-of-a-kind songs for them.

John got busy gathering a team of songwriters and performers across the country to compose and record the unique songs. Songs of Love, the only non-profit organization of its kind, was founded shortly afterwards and now has a volunteer group of over 350 talented artists.

Collaborating with some 150 hospitals, private health-care institutions, and with various individual families, they have produced intimate musical portraits for over 1,200 children and teens. Every week, Songs of Love receives numerous letters attesting to the therapeutic effect these custom-made songs have had on the youngsters who are often undergoing lengthy and painful treatment. Parents, guardians, hospital staff, and, most importantly, the children themselves, share their heartfelt stories about what an amazing gift the songs are and how much they have helped.

Here are some testimonies to Songs of Love, reprinted with permission from their website:

"Whenever I am feeling down or having a bad day, I like to listen to my song 'cause it says all the good stuff about me. My mom surprised me with the song. That day I didn't feel happy. When I heard the song it cheered me up. I was so happy it brought tears to my eyes. I am writing this letter to let you know how happy I am 'cause of this song. Thank you." *—Caleb Kenison, Age 13*

"I'm writing this to thank you for the beautiful song you wrote for our Jordan. Sometimes at night when she's in a lot of pain, we play her song and it helps to calm her and put her at peace." *—Jordan's mother*

"Thank you so much for the beautiful tape for my daughter Katie. She was diagnosed with Leukemia on August 20th, 1997. She has literally cried every time she has received injections for blood draws and medicines. The play therapist (Trudy) in Children's Hospital gave Katie her tape to listen to while going through one of these procedures on Friday, and for the very first time she did not cry! It was an answer to our prayers. She loves her special tape and plays it over and over! Words cannot express my gratitude of thanks to you! She says she is going to play it every time she goes in for treatment. Thank you from the bottom of our hearts!" *—Katie's parents*

"How do you type a smile? How do you show the sunshine of happiness on a piece of paper? Pamela, who is in the advanced stages of Huntington's Disease, is so depressed that all the gifts and cards I bring her seem to produce little reaction. Your song gave her such joy that she wanted me to play it over and over again. I visit Pam every week in the nursing home where she resides. I will bring it with me each time so she will know that she is loved and not forgotten." *—Pamela's mother*

"Your special songs written just for individual children are one of the most effective ways to boost spirits, raise self-esteem, and promote the positive feelings necessary to cope with hospitalization and chronic illness." *—Nicole Miller, Wyler Children's Hospital*

"It is no coincidence that Apollo was the god of both music and medicine in ancient Greece. Today, we have empirical evidence that music is often a useful adjunct in the treatment of numerous disease states, and we have angels from Songs of Love to bring music to suffering children and adults one-by-one." *—Mark Jude Tramo, M.D., Ph.D., Harvard Medical School & Massachusetts General Hospital Director, Institute for Music and Brain Science*

"The very first 'Song of Love' I ever wrote was for 5-year-old Brittany who had cancer. Her mother put her on the phone, and with the cutest little voice she simply said, 'Thank you for my song.' After that defining moment, there was no turning back! Since its inception in February of 1996, Songs of Love has produced over 1,900 songs for more than 150 hospitals across the United States. The pool of volunteers has grown to over 350 songwriters, singers and instrumentalists who are extremely excited about being able to give back with the talents they have been given.   *—John Beltzer, President, Songs of Love Foundation*

HARMONIOUS FACT: Singing therapy has been used to help autistic children learn to speak. The students begin by singing a song, then work on slowing the phrases down until they become normal speech patterns.

TEN WAYS TO SING AND PROMOTE HEALING

(Always consult your doctor before making any changes in your personal health program.)

1. When Helen Fruth sings, her confusion and anxiety from Alzheimer's disease lessen. Singing allows children and their Alzheimer parents to be together again, if only for the duration of a song. Continuing with singing during daily chores, such as getting dressed, can turn such tasks into games rather than challenges. *Sing with Alzheimer patients and diminish their confusion.*

2. James Hill, a member of the legendary gospel group, the Fairfield Four, has arthritis, but when he sings, it never bothers him. A mother in labor discovered there was no pain while she sang. A gentleman in the 1930s joined in a community sing and forgot about his toothache. *Sing and stop the pain.*

3. Barbershop singing groups discover that they must work on their muscles as regards breathing and posture all the time. Maintaining the perfect stance with weight on the balls of the feet, sternum up, rib cage up and expanded, knees unlocked, shoulders comfortable, and no tension in the throat, neck, or jaw results in positive posture habits for life. *Sing and improve your posture.*

4. According to physiology professors, singing in the shower is a great stress-buster. Using the lungs to full capacity, deeply breathing in and out relaxes the body and lowers blood pressure. *Sing and reduce stress.*

5. A study by the University of California, Irvine, found that choral singing boosts the production of antibodies that fight disease. The levels of one antibody increased 150 percent after the reheasals and 240 percent after the performance. ***Sing with others and promote your immunity to disease.***

6. Dr. Carl Winter of the UC Davis Food Safe Program puts critical information about toxicology into song parodies to make valuable information easier to assimilate. ***Sing and remember helpful health information.***

7. Germs are kept at bay with good handwashing. Use soap and hot water and wash for at least 20 seconds. How do you know whether you've washed long enough? Sing "Happy Birthday". One chorus of this popular song will remind you to keep washing and time your completion of the process. ***Sing and stop germs.***

8. Psychologically disturbed patients, unable to express their confused feelings, listen to songs by popular artists who have also suffered from internal torments, and sing back the songs to initiate discussion. ***Sing and start the psychological healing process.***

9. Veteran Joseph Pearl kept Parkinson's Disease at bay for three years by singing the tune to "Bridge on the River Kwai." Singing that song gave him courage to enlist in World War II despite his age, kept him climbing during maneuvers, and kept him out of a wheelchair when illness struck. ***Sing and beat back disease.***

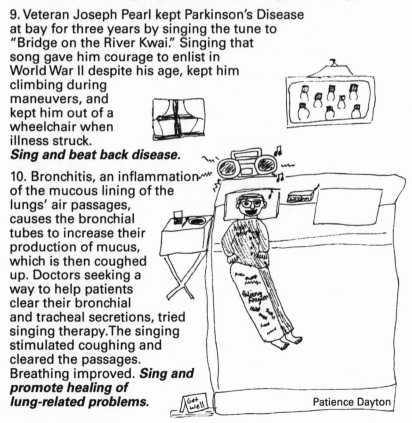

10. Bronchitis, an inflammation of the mucous lining of the lungs' air passages, causes the bronchial tubes to increase their production of mucus, which is then coughed up. Doctors seeking a way to help patients clear their bronchial and tracheal secretions, tried singing therapy. The singing stimulated coughing and cleared the passages. Breathing improved. ***Sing and promote healing of lung-related problems.***

Patience Dayton

Sing and Stop the Pain

(Sung to "Singing in the Rain")

Sing and stop the pain.
Just sing and stop the pain.
Get rid of the toothache and feel good again.
Got an earache? Then sing.
In labor? Then sing.
Arthritis? Try singing...and stop the pain.

Sing to Beat Your Limitations

(Sung to "I've Been Working on the Railroad")

Sing to beat your limitations.
Sing and overcome a stroke.
Sing to loosen up a stutter
That causes words to choke.

Sing though you may lack a language.
Sing through aphasia.
Sing to overcome autism.
Sing to block seizure!

VI.

SING AND SOLVE A PROBLEM

The Woman in the Concentration Camp

In the Academy-Award-Winning movie *Life Is Beautiful*, a family is separated, but contained within a single concentration camp. How can the husband communicate to the wife that he and their son are still alive? Fortunately, the husband is serving as a waiter for the evening and has access to a record player. He turns it toward the window and puts on an opera. The song, wafting out into the fog, is "The Merry Widow," the favorite opera of his wife—the opera playing the night he captured her heart. She hears the singing through a window of the barracks. The song verifies the husband's existence and gives the wife the hope and will to survive. Their communication problem has been solved by an opera star singing a song.

Can singing solve problems?

Here are Beethoven, Martin Luther, and Davy Crockett to prove that it can. But first, a word from Merle Levy, who kept her ailing baby awake —and alive— with a song.

David Francis Dayton

DEAR DAVID,

WHEN OUR YOUNGEST, ETHAN, WAS BORN, HIS TRACHEA WAS NOT FULLY DEVELOPED. THIS LED TO BOTH BREATHING AND FEEDING PROBLEMS IN INFANCY. HE DIDN'T HAVE THE ABILITY TO SUCK AND BREATHE AT THE SAME TIME, AND WOULD EXHAUST HIMSELF TRYING TO DRINK BABY FORMULA. FALLING ASLEEP BEFORE HE GOT ENOUGH NOURISHMENT AND NOT BEING ABLE TO HOLD DOWN WHAT HE DID GET WAS FRUSTRATING AND POTENTIALLY DANGEROUS.

OUR PEDIATRICIAN ADVISED US TO ADD BABY CEREAL TO THE FORMULA AND FEED HIM IN A SITTING POSITION — UNORTHODOX FOR THE TIME. IT WAS IMPERATIVE THAT HE FINISH EVERY BOTTLE BECAUSE HE HAD ALREADY LOST PRECIOUS OUNCES DURING THE DIAGNOSTIC PROCESS.

THE SITTING POSITION WAS AWKWARD AT FIRST, AND ATTRACTED MORE THAN A FEW STARES, AND KEEPING ETHAN AWAKE WAS A CONSTANT BATTLE.

INSTINCTIVELY, I BEGAN SINGING TO KEEP ETHAN STIMULATED. THE FIRST SONG THAT POPPED OUT WAS "YOU CAN DO IT" FROM WALT DISNEY'S "CINDERELLA." HOLDING ETHAN IN AN UPRIGHT POSITION, I SANG THIS TINY INFANT BACK TO HEALTH. TO THIS DAY, WHEN ETHAN, NOW AN ACTIVE 12-YEAR-OLD, DOESN'T WANT TO FINISH A MEAL, I CATCH MYSELF SINGING "YOU CAN DO IT!"

SINCERELY,

38. Remember the Alamo (c. 1836)

Whenever I feel afraid...I whistle a happy tune.
—Oscar Hammerstein II

If you grew up during the fifties, you probably know that Davy Crockett wore a coonskin cap, fought Indians, and died at the Alamo. If you ever heard "The Ballad of Davy Crockett," you might recall the frontiersman "kilt him a bar when he was only three" and "patched up the crack in the liberty bell." But whatever tall tales or short facts anyone shared with you about Colonel Crockett, chances are no one told you about his most sublime moment—the time he saved the valor of two hundred men by singing a tender song.

Davy Crockett started life in a log cabin built at the mouth of Limestone Creek in the green hills of Tennessee. His patriotic elders fought British redcoats and disgruntled Indians. Crockett pioneered his profession as an Indian fighter, but later broke ranks to become an Indian rights activist.

After six months of frontier-quality education, he quit school at twelve to drive cattle to Virginia. While in Virginia, he grew into an expert marksman by practicing with borrowed guns. He returned home at fifteen, six feet tall, and paid off all his father's debts before setting out in new clothes on a new horse, with a new rifle named Betsy.

Following his personal motto "Be sure you're right, then go ahead," newly appointed Colonel Crocket took command of a battalion in the Creek Indian War in 1813-1814. He ran for office and represented Tennessee in Congress. He wrote up his autobiography for popular distribution. But he wrote no songs.

Meanwhile, the Texans cried for liberty. They captured San Antonio in 1835, but left only 144 soldiers to guard the city under the temper of Lt. Colonel W. B. Travis. On February 22, 1836, General Santa Ana arrived with a force of five thousand Mexican troops. Travis and Colonel James Bowie argued over leadership, but both agreed the Alamo must be held to prevent Santa Ana from marching into the interior. Giving up politics for good, Davy Crockett and his Tennessee

Mounted Volunteers arrived just after the general. The rag-tag mountain men joined the forces in the fort, and prepared to withstand an attack by the Mexicans.

The Alamo never pretended to be a true fort. The Spanish settlers raised the adobe-clay structure as a vocational school to educate Indians in cattle raising, weaving, carpentry, and stone masonry. How many Indians graduated with a degree in cattle-raising is not known.

The once-upon-a-time Catholic mission spread over three acres with a surrounding stone wall twelve feet high and three feet thick. The roofless chapel meditated in the south east corner, facing west. A two-story structure called the long barracks blocked up the east side of the Alamo and contained the crumbling convent and hospital.

The fort boasted twenty-one pieces of artillery, a good supply of British Brown Bess muskets with sixteen thousand rounds of ammunition, and frontier hero Davy Crockett.

Outside the Alamo, General Santa Ana raised a flag of no quarter. The Texans had defeated his brother-in-law and tainted the family honor. Santa Ana sought redemption. He demanded unconditional surrender.

The Texans answered with a cannon shot over the Mexican camp.

The general vowed revenge without mercy.

If the volunteers could hold the Alamo, San Antonio might become a rallying point for all of Texas and the cause of Independence. But the Alamo required one thousand men to successfully defend its walls. The militia inside numbered 150.

Thirty-two more fighters arrived from Gonzales with James Butler Bonham.

On the night of March the fifth, Davy Crockett and his Tennessee Mounted Volunteers stood duty in the worst spot of the defense—the wooden palisade between the church and the low barracks, a fifty-yard gap fortified with earth and logs. Crockett looked out over the space dividing the ocean of Mexican infantry from the puddle of Texans inside the pottery of the Alamo.

He wondered how he and the volunteers could best prepare to meet the massacre, which would begin in the morning.

A prayer?

No priests or preachers remained among them.

A rousing speech?

Travis and Bowie had talked them to death.

The man in the coonskin cap cocked his rifle, rested his elbow, and thought. Then he knew.

The battle of March the Sixth has been documented. Several thousand shouting Mexicans poured over the Alamo with bayonets charging. Colonel Travis died swearing at the north wall. Defenders breaking through the attackers met powder and shot on the field from the cavalry. Mexican troops seized control of the fortress and jeered as they fired the fort's own cannons point-blank into the barracks. Invaders bayoneted Colonel Bowie on his sickbed and tossed him like a bale of hay.

Down came the heavy doors of the church, battered apart by the swarming army of Santa Ana. When ammunition ran out, Davy Crockett skull-cracked more enemy with the butt of his rifle than he had clipped with his bullets. After brief hand-to-hand combat, the last defenders fell.

The wounded were murdered and the dead mutilated. Revenge without mercy. But the moments before the battle have also been remembered.

A woman—one of the thirty noncombatants at the Alamo—recalled that the King of the Wild Frontier stood at his post on the adobe wall in the morning cold and kept the fort at peace with Irish verse:

Will you come to the bow'r o'er the free boundless ocean—where the stupendous waves roll in thundering motion—where the mermaids are seen and the fierce tempest gathers—to loved Erin the green, the dearland of our fathers...

Davy Crockett—red-blooded, crack-shot, bear-wrestling, Indian-fighting yarn-spinning hero of the American frontier calmed the defenders' nerves before the charge and saved the valor of the Alamo... by singing a heart-felt ballad.

HARMONIOUS FACT: Singing can relieve stress and reduce fear. If you suffer from any of the ten most common fears, try singing a related song:

1. Arachnophobia (fear of spiders): Sing "Itsy Bitsy Spider."
2. Sociophobia (fear of people or social situations): Sing "People" from *Funny Girl*.
3. Aerophobia (fear of flying): Sing "You Can Fly" from *Peter Pan*.
4. Agoraphobia (fear of open spaces): Sing "Don't Fence Me In."
5. Claustrophobia (fear of confined spaces): Sing "It's a Small World."
6. Emetophobia (fear of vomiting): Sing "Everything's Coming Up Roses" from *Gypsy*.
7. Acrophobia (fear of heights): Sing "Let's Go Fly a Kite."
8. Cancerphobia (fear of cancer): Sing "Amazing Grace."
9. Brontophobia (fear of thunderstorms): Sing "My Favorite Things."
10. Necrophobia (fear of death): Sing "A Lot of Livin' to Do" from *Bye, Bye Birdie*.

MAY 31, 2000

DEAR MR. DAYTON:

EACH THURSDAY NIGHT, AT OUR INN IN LOS OLIVOS, MY WIFE AND I SHARE SINGING AND MUSIC WITH OUR GUESTS. MY WIFE IS IN THE PROCESS OF RECORDING A CD CALLED "AN EVENING IN MARCY PARKER'S LIVING ROOM WITH BILL POWELL AT THE PIANO." MUSIC IS INDEED A VERY SPECIAL PART OF OUR LIVES.

THANK YOU FOR YOUR INTEREST AND BEST OF LUCK WITH YOUR BOOK.

SINCERELY,

FESS PARKER

39. The Girl Who Sang for America (c. 1925)

My country 'tis of thee, sweet land of liberty, of thee I sing.
—Samuel Francis Smith

Were you born and bred in the USA?

Do you take your citizenship for granted?

Jean Fritz does not.

Jean Fritz is an award-winning writer. She is a non-fiction author who has written on a dozen American history topics and completed dozens of American biographies. She won the Boston Globe Horn Book Honor Book Award, 1980, for *Stonewall*. She grabbed an American Book Award nomination, 1981, for *Traitor: The Case of Benedict Arnold*. And she won the Boston Globe Horn Book Nonfiction Award, 1984, for *The Double Life of Pocahontas*. Her biography subjects include George Washington, Patrick Henry, Paul Revere, Benjamin Franklin, Abraham Lincoln, Sam Houston, Teddy Roosevelt, and Christopher Columbus. In fact, Jean Fritz may be the preeminent nonfiction children's author on American subjects and American characters. This may be somewhat startling since Jean Fritz was born November 16, 1915, in Hankow, China.

Jean's parents were American missionaries. Jean's mother gave birth thousands of miles from her native country. In spite of living in China, Jean grew up loving every story her father told her of homeland USA.

Maybe that explains why Jean spent the rest of her life researching the history of the United States and turning history into best-selling, award-winning children's books. Maybe that explains why Jean became one of the best writers of American biographies and novels for young people.

She had to.

She grew up hungry for home.

Life in China gave Jean one set of problems. Her elementary school gave her another. Jean woke up each morning, put on her school clothes, and marched off to learn from the British.

At least her teachers spoke English. But they were British, and being British, they promoted British ways. American student Jean had to adapt to those British ways.

The British teacher and the British class started the British school day by singing the rousing national anthem, "God Save the King." The problem was, Jean did not want to save the King. She did not want to have anything to do with the King. She was an American and proud of it.

But Jean was also ten years old. Ten-year-old girls have spirit, but not many rights. Especially ten-year-old American girls in a British school. In Hankow, China, in 1925.

First she asked her mother to write her an excuse. "When in Rome," said her mother, "do as the Romans do."

Second, she tried to fake it. She simply closed her mouth and hoped no one would notice. Someone did. The teacher. "Is there something wrong with your voice today, Jean?" she asked.

The exposure of the non-singing American proved damaging. Jean fought with the school bully, who happened to be British and loved to sing, especially about his king. He ground his heavy heels into her toes and twisted her arm, but she refused even to say the words of the foreign anthem. A game started, and the bully left for the game, but Jean knew he would be back with his heavy heels tomorrow.

Jean cried her heart out at home, hoping her mother would give in and homeschool her. Or at least send her back to live with Grandma in America. Anything to avoid the pain and humiliation of returning to the British school.

But mother was sensible. "Go back tomorrow and sing."

Father was the revolutionary in the family. Jean turned to him. Father sat down at the piano solemnly and plunked out the tune to "God Save the King."

The ten-year-old American girl felt betrayed. Everyone was against her. She prepared to burst into tears again...until she heard her father singing a song by Samuel Francis Smith.

Jean attended school the next day. Jean sang in school the next day. But while the British students sang out their proud British hearts, no one noticed that Jean Fritz sang something just a little bit different—the song she heard her father singing—the song written by Samuel Francis Smith.

Apparently, Samuel Francis Smith held the same devotion for America as Jean Fritz. But he did not share the same aversion to "God Save the King." In fact, he loved "God Save the King." He loved it so much, he stole the whole tune, note for note, and used it to score his new patriotic hymn which premiered on July 4th, 1832.

Good old patriotic Samuel Francis Smith. Jean should write a biography about him. He saved her honor that next day in school. For while the British students sang "God Save the King," Jean sang the song her father sang, the song written by Samuel Francis Smith—"My Country 'Tis of Thee" Different words from different countries, written to the same tune.

Jean Fritz saved her patriotic pride and solved her problem by singing a different song.

HARMONIOUS FACT: In 1938, Irving Berlin retrieved a song from a drawer for the world's last Armistice Day. "God Bless America" could not stop the war, but it carried America through it. And all proceeds from singing the song contributed to the financial support of the Boy and Girl Scouts.

40. Singing to Save a Dead Man (c. 457)

Good night sweet prince and a flight of angels sing thee to thy rest.
—Shakespeare

Fans can be fanatical. The twentieth century saw movie stars and rock singers mobbed by the thousands. Most were lucky to lose only a shirt or a bit of hair.

In the fifth century, however, fans wanted body parts.

In the Roman world, slavery ran as a legitimate business. Each foreign battle brought fresh captives designated for sale to the barbarians. Bishop Deogratias hated slavery. He sold off every bit of silver and gold in his church to buy freedom for Roman chattel before the poor souls fell into the hands of the Vandals and Moors.

His generosity and personal holiness built an audience of admirers. They proclaimed him a saint at death. And at death everyone wanted a memento of holiness. This could mean big business for the proprietors of Carthage. They plotted to tear his remains into pieces to obtain multiple saleable relics. The good bishop's true disciples held other plans.

When the fans and plotters and parishioners gathered in the church, the disciples prepared for a secret burial. The officiating priest began the mass—a requiem mass, a singing mass. The singing gave the disciples all the time they needed. While the fans sang joyously on behalf of their beloved saint, and the plotters sang joyfully in anticipation of their relic sales, the disciples smuggled the corpse out of the church and secretly buried it.

St. Deogratias' body survived mutilation thanks to his fans' fanatic singing. Another problem solved by singing a song.

HARMONIOUS FACT: St. Botvid's murdered body lay on a vessel drifting lost in the fog. Then a bird settled on the boat and sang until the search party arrived. Disciples of the "Apostle of Sweden" removed his body and gave it a proper sacramental interment.

---

41. Singing for Daily Bread (c. 1906)

Little Tommy Tucker sings for his supper.
—Mother Goose

Father—a part-time Baptist preacher—died when she was born. Mother died before she reached ten.

Her oldest sister, Viola, took responsibility for the family upon her shoulders. She moved the children into a tenement apartment in Tannery Flats, the poverty corner of Chattanooga, Tennessee. Black women in the South at the turn-of-the-century washed clothes for the rich. Viola took in laundry.

Oldest brother Clarence worked whatever odd job he could. That brought in a little money. Then he left town to strike out on his own, and the little money left with him.

Then came our heroine's turn. What could she do to help the family, which numbered as many as seven brothers and sisters with no mother and no father? Too small to wash laundry. Too small for odd jobs. She took to the street with a younger brother and collected the coins people threw at them.

The nine-year-old girl took a cue from Little Tommy Tucker. She sang for her family's supper.

She continued to sing, week after week, month after month. Within a few years, the young girl singing for her daily bread sang her way into a career and a title.

"Empress of the Blues" Bessie Smith started on a street corner, singing to help her family survive.

HARMONIOUS FACT: George Bernard Shaw's mother sang a new style of singing lessons to feed the family when father Shaw departed.

===

42. Roll Out the Barrel (c. 1939)

Every sickness is a musical problem, every cure a musical solution.
—Novalis

Near the beginning of World War II, British prisoners stood in a muddy prison-camp yard listening to the loudspeaker pipe out German radio broadcasts. In German-English, the broadcaster clamored out the most recent raids on London and detailed the successful bombing. A fatherland song of political conquest followed the dismal newscast.

As the Nazi Party victory march blasted out across the barbed wire and echoed in the heads of the downed British pilots, the air grew colder and blacker.

"London is dying," proclaimed the voice.

"England is lost," proclaimed the voice.

"The Fatherland over all!" announced the German song of conquest.

One officer refused to listen.

Instead, he staged a protest—by singing.

Roll out the barrel! We'll have a barrel of fun!

Insane. Nonsensical.

Until the singing protest caught on.

Another officer joined in—a duet. A third bellowed out—a trio. A fourth, a fifth, a dozen, a hundred, five hundred.

The Nazi Party march song shrank into insignificance under the power of the polka that barreled through the camp, shook the windows, echoed off the stockades and snapped the guards' eardrums.

Life turned into a musical.

A British alehouse song met, challenged, and conquered the might of the German propaganda machine. The pilots crushed short term fears with the elation of a song.

HARMONIOUS FACT: For four weeks, five times a week, music therapists worked with men at a veteran's hospital suffering from Alzheimer's and related mental conditions. Men locked inside their brains, unable or unwilling to communicate, suddenly opened up when involved in singing. One man liked show tunes, another liked opera, still another responded to Cuban folk songs. One closed-mouth admiral broke forth with all the verses to a bawdy version of "Anchors Aweigh," then closed back up when the music stopped. Even so, singing opened the mouths and minds of men lost in a permanent fog.

But an even more astonishing result came from the singing. The researchers took blood-test results weeks after the sessions ended and discovered the melatonin levels of the patients had risen 400 percent.

Sing and free minds trapped in Alzheimer's. Sing and heal bodies trapped by disease. Sing and give prisoners hope.

Sarah Dayton

43. Just As I Am (c.1880)

A song will outlive sermons in the memory.
—Anonymous

Charlotte Elliot must have felt a million miles from success.

Her brother, Harry, wanted to build a college in Brighton and the whole family planned to help. They would put together a bazaar to raise the money—then raise the building off the ground.

Unfortunately, Charlotte Elliot could not help with the bazaar. She lay sick in bed, straddled with illness, too ill to lift more than an arm.

As things turned out, however, an arm was all she needed—along with a voice.

Singing would help her overcome her limitations.

Lying in bed, staring out the window, Charlotte started mumbling, "Just as I am. Jesus can use me just as I am." Inspired, she took a pen and began to write from her heart until she completed a hymn.

A hymn now known the world over as "Just As I Am."

With one voice, one arm, and one song, Charlotte raised more money than the entire family. "Just As I Am" sold so many copies, it brought in more proceeds than the whole bazaar, and has since sold more than 100 bazaars.

All Charlotte Elliot wanted to do was help the family project in spite of physical limitations; she contributed the most by writing and singing a song.

HARMONIOUS FACT: Billy Graham made his altar call when the choir sang "Just As I Am." The song made such an impact on him, he decided to use it when he began his crusades.

---

44. The Song Symphony (c. 1827)

Everything ends in songs.
—Beaumarchais

When you think *symphony*, an orchestra might come to mind. After all, a symphony is a musical composition for an orchestra, not singers.

Or is it?

Most symphonies have four movements. The first is fast, the second is slow, the third has a dance-like quality, and the fourth is a lively or triumphant conclusion.

Joseph Haydn wrote more than one hundred symphonies in the 1700s and solidified the symphony into a major musical form. Wolfgang Amadeus Mozart took the symphony and refined it into an elegant form now recognized as the classical symphony. Yet composers of the 1800s and early 1900s looked back neither at Haydn nor Mozart for their symphonic form. They followed the direction of Ludwig Van Beethoven.

Beethoven wrote nine symphonies. He gave the third his heroic spirit. He gave the fifth his defiance of fate. He gave the sixth his love of nature. He paid tribute to victory in the seventh. In the ninth he would achieve and speak his ultimate symphonic message.

How important is Beethoven's Ninth Symphony?

Consider this.

The standard capacity of a CD is approximately seventy four minutes. This standard was chosen because it was long enough for an entire performance of Beethoven's Ninth Symphony, a symphony "recognized as one of the all-time greatest achievements, not just in music, but for humanity as a whole." (Milestones of the Millenium)

What happens in this symphony to distinguish it from all others?

Three grand movements are heard. Some say it is the description of God creating the world out of chaos, bringing order out of a fallen universe. When the fourth and final movement begins, the exuberant theme takes off in the violins. Surely the listeners will be swept up in what is one of Beethoven's simplest, yet most beloved melodies.

No. The grand sonata scheme is abandoned, interrupted by a timpani roll and followed by an orchestral shriek—the same wild holler of orchestra that started the fourth movement.

Are we plunged back into chaos? Is this Beethoven's final word to humanity? Life rises only to fall again?

All instruments cease. Then, a single baritone voice exclaims, *O Freunde, nict diese Teine!* (O friends, no more these sounds!) The symphony leaps up to a higher level. It is humanity's finest musical hour. A choir of voices enters like angels from the heavens.

How did Beethoven consummate the symphonic moment of his career and of all history? How did he solve the problem of the perfect ending?

He crowned his masterpiece with the finishing exaltation of the singing human voice. He solved his musical problem and finished his Ninth with a song.

HARMONIOUS FACT: Composer Jean Baptiste Lully first worked as a servant in a fine lady's kitchen, then moved to her private orchestra when his musical talent became apparent. As a lowly musician, he could not easily leave to find a better position, so he wrote and sang a song about his patron that displeased her so much she kicked him out of the house just in time for him to apply for a position with the King. Singing about his employer improved his employment.

---

45. The Devil Made Him Do It (c. 1520)

*(Hildegard of Bingen's) idea seems to be that singing reflects
harmony and harmony reflects the glory of God,
therefore the Devil doesn't sing.*
—Eve Beglarian

The candle goes out.

Blown by the wind?

Martin turns from his desk to see a figure in the corner of his moonlit room. Who assails a man in his own room? "I have nothing," says Martin. "I am a monk. I have taken the vow of poverty."

"I know who you are," laughs the figure.

The laugh unnerves Martin. The laugh is not the laugh of a man. There is something inhuman, even unearthly, in its tone. "And I know who you are!" thunders Martin.

A loud snarl erupts from the figure in the corner. A foul stench blows across the room. The thing in the room rises up high as the ceiling, then crouches for an attack. "You are the devil!" declares Martin. "And I bid you be gone."

"I am the devil," agrees the figure. "And I shall stay."

A thousand thoughts fly through the monk's mind. Shall he call for help? Shall he spout Scripture? Shall he fall on his knees and beg deliverance from God?

Inspiration strikes. The monk opens his mouth and sings.

A hymn of devotion and prayer drives the devil away. Martin Luther turns back to his work, having solved the problem of demonic attack with a song.

HARMONIOUS FACT: Sixties rock singer Arthur Brown called himself the "god of hellfire" in his hit song of the time. Now he works with a licensed counselor to help people deal with everything from depression to substance abuse. Brown listens in on the session, writes a song based on the discussion, and sings it back to the patient via tape. The singing leads to insight and healing for the patient.

---

46. Puritan Teenagers (c. 1600)

*To this day, I don't understand how people think they can
bring anybody together without a song.*
—Bernice Johnson Reagon

How much fun can a Puritan have?

Imagine those Puritan teenagers. No rock and roll. No
movies. No CDs. No malls. No cars. And the Puritan religion
restricted other possibilities. No dances. No make-up. No
parties.

What could Puritan teenagers do to make and keep
friends? Well, they all collected in a big room or barn and sat
in a circle. Then they readied their hands for a clapping game.

And they sang. That is all they had, but singing pulled
them through.

Puritan teenagers solved the problem of making friends
by singing songs.

HARMONIOUS FACT: Some psychotherapists suggest interacting
with your teenagers through song, rather than sternly raising your
voice. Instead of yelling, sing your request: "Please don't shout
and please don't pout. Just do your chores and then go out."

---

47. The People Who Sang Up Deer (c. 1000)

Men, even when alone, lighten their labors by song.
—Quintilian

The Cherokee Indians commanded more than forty thousand square miles of land in the southern Appalachians by 1650. They successfully assimilated white culture after 1800, redesigning their government, adapting new methods of farming, and adopting new modes of dress.

Cherokee culture flourished in 1821 with the invention of the Cherokee syllabary, which made possible a written Cherokee constitution and the publication of the only Native American newspaper, *The Cherokee Phoenix*. Then gold was discovered in Georgia, the U.S. government passed the "Indian Removal Act" and, within a decade, the Cherokee "Enchanted Land" nation disappeared.

Such is the unpleasant history of the United States. But drop back before the Europeans arrived. How did those first Cherokee survive so well in a land that killed off most of the first white settlers?

Survival is a struggle between life and death. It begins with getting enough sustenance for a day. Those who survive the day can tackle the turns of the seasons and conquer the years. Then they can pass on their knowledge to future generations.

How did the Cherokee survive the day? The women and children gathered. The men hunted.

Picture the hunters out in the woods waiting for game. They could wait a long time for a deer to come obligingly along. So they carried another weapon with them besides the bow and arrow. To attract potential dinner, the Cherokee sang a deer song.

It must have worked well because the Cherokee braves survived not just a day or a season, but passed along the deer song to all younger generations—for a thousand years.

HARMONIOUS FACT: After the Civil War, Union General James J. Carleston attacked a tribe of Navajos and unjustly imprisoned them. The Navajo women followed their husbands and boys to the compound and chanted the "Navajo Happiness Song" day and night to keep up their spirits. The song prevailed; the warriors refrained from escalating the incident, and the federal government stepped in to release them.

48. The Reluctant Bride (c. 177)

Song wins grace with the gods above, and with the gods below.
—Horace

Cecilia lived ahead of her time.

Eighteen hundred years ahead.

Her father made all the customary arrangements for her marriage. It was the economically sensible thing to do.

Cecilia was not economically sensible. She resounded with the idealism of youth. She took a Chrisitan vow to remain a virgin and consecrated herself to God. Did she share her vow with her father? Well, if she did, he gave it no notice. Father set the marriage date and sent out the wedding invitations.

The organ played, the white-robed wedding guests sang, the groom beamed, and Cecilia's father burst with pride. Everyone oozed happiness except the bride. The excitement, noise and festivity swelled into a tide of rushing chords, drowning the girl's quiet sobbing in a riot of celebration.

Then the idealistic Cecilia decided to fight back—with singing. Her song began low and hidden, but it sailed from her heart and soared straight to God. She sang for His grace, His miracles, and His Spirit to give her the right words to say to a rich Roman groom steeped in the pagan culture.

The ceremony ended. The guests left. Cecilia and her spouse squared off alone. Cecilia spoke out with song-filled faith.

"If you touch me," she announced to her pagan groom, Valerian, "an angel will strike you down." Thus did the honeymoon begin.

Valerian did not give up so easily. "Let me see the angel," he requested.

Cecilia sang another song of faith to God.

Valerian saw the angel—and the light.

The pagan groom submitted to baptism, became a Christian, and devoted himself to a celibate marriage of good works. When Valerian's pagan brother, Tiburtius, stopped by to see how the newlyweds were coming along, he was at first astounded. Then Cecilia sang to God on his behalf and he, too, converted.

In Cecilia's world, being a Christian meant being a martyr. The bodies of martyrs received no respect. So Valerian and Tiburtius set off with a song in their hearts to bury their Christian comrades. The two brothers soon became martyrs themselves.

Cecilia buried her husband, then her brother-in-law, before meeting her own similar fate. Yet, through it all, she kept her idealism and her Christian vow of celibacy thanks to singing a song from her soul.

She now sings from heaven as patroness of music and singing, encouraging those on earth to solve their problems with a prayer and a song.

HARMONIOUS FACT: Paul Dresser (brother of American author Theodore Dreiser) once wrote "The Curse of the Dreamer" and sang it to his estranged wife to effect a successful, though short-term, reconciliation.

---

49. The Jubilee Singers (c. 1871)

All this for a song!
—William Cecil

The Jubilee Singers needed something unusual to sing. Their classical songs could not attract an audience large enough to pay their bills. And their bills amounted to two thousand dollars—in 1864.

After the Civil War, in 1864, John Ogden, Reverend Erastus Mio Cravath, and Reverend Edward P. Smith established the Fisk School in Nashville. They named the school in honor of General Clinton B. Fisk who provided the institution with facilities in former Union army barracks.

The students were ex-slaves who wanted to learn, and saw education as furthering the emancipation that the Civil War struggle had only begun.

Six years later, Fisk University faced closure. The buildings were in desperate need of repairs, food was scare, teachers could not afford to be kept on, and local debts reached the breaking point. Not even outside financial support from the Freedmen's Bureau and the American Missionary Association could sustain the school.

Then the treasurer of the University, George L. White, got an idea.

He collected some of the best singers on the campus and trained them in classic songs for the purpose of giving concerts across the country to raise money for the school. They marched into the fray as the Fisk Singers.

At first the group had modest success. George and his troop of eleven valiantly sang across Ohio. Alas, the meager earnings would not justify their continuance.

So, during the tours of Ohio, the singers changed their program and exploded in popularity. White thanked the Lord for their success and received a revelation. He announced to the troupe, "Children, God has given you a name—you shall be called the Jubilee Singers."

The freshly christened Fisk Jubilee Singers, with their

changed program, finished off the Midwest and set out for New York, Pennsylvania, New Jersey, Massachusetts and Connecticut. At last they reached Washington D.C. where a very appreciative President Ulysses S. Grant invited them to sing at the White House.

Their first season of cross-country singing netted twenty thousand dollars, more than enough to pay the school debts and expand the University.

White made arrangements for a European tour. No more nonsense about classical music. The Fisk Jubilee Singers sang their own special program and garnered praise across the globe. In Glasgow and Edinburgh, seventy-five hundred workmen gathered to hear them sing at a "praise meeting."

They sang in hospitals, prisons, and the streets. They sang to the poor, to the rich, and to all those between. The singers made history as the first black singing group to perform before the crowned heads of Europe.

What made them so successful?

What change of program could have produced such a difference in the reception these ex-slaves received in the United States and eventually the world?

Instead of classic songs, the Fisk Jubilee Singers went back to their roots. They brought back over fifty thousand dollars from Europe by singing the songs they learned as slaves. Singing the songs of poverty and servitude enriched their foundations for the future.

HARMONIOUS FACT: Renaissance university students in Spain sang in the streets to raise money for their tuition and books.

---

50. Singing in a Cave (c. 1980)

O give us the man who sings at his work!
—Thomas Carlyle

Large animals—prehistoric horses, stoneage cattle, ancient bison, ice-age deer and the famous wooly mammoths—drew the eyes of the prehistoric painter. Lumps of charcoal or colored pigments of maganese or ocher could be scratched across a cave wall to depict the beasts roaming above. The realists of the prehistoric age must have carried all their materials with them, and some source of light, for almost all of the paintings are "hanging" deeply buried in dark and almost inaccessible parts of subterranean caves.

French art expert Andre Leroi-Gourhan took a statistical approach to prehistoric cave paintings and systematically categorized practically the whole of European Paleolithic cave art. He came up with this distribution of animal figures: 610 horses, 510 bison, 205 mammoths, 175 rhinos, nine nondescript monsters, eight large-horned deer, eight fish, six birds, three nondescript beasts of prey, two wild boars, and two chamoix.

Most of the cave paintings are in France and Spain, but a good showing of the ancient artists does appear in caves under Italian and Portuguese soil. The technique in most cases seems to have been to outline the beast on the wall in charcoal, then brush or blow on the earth paints. Conscious of their profession, the artists signed their works with hand prints.

The works have been on display for about fifteen thousand years, though some Paleolithics put forth a good showing of their artistry about thirty thousand years ago. The medium died out between eight thousand and three thousand B.C. when artists turned to walls and pottery to display their talents.

Many guesses have been ventured as to the purpose of the paintings. Magical or religious aids to hunting? Secret initiation rites? There is some evidence of one being used as a doctor's office. The first pictures depicting spinal manipulation were discovered in prehistoric cave paintings in Point le Merd in southwestern France dating back to 17,500 B.C. Perhaps many were painted just to relieve the urge of the artist to recreate the world and all its wondrous creatures.

Imagine discovering one of these prehistoric caves — dropping down into the earth's crust, squeezing between shoulders of rock, and entering the chill of an underground cavern. The ceilings crush down, the walls press in until claustrophobia seeps through the pores of your skin. You are crawling about in the unending black, unless you brought along your flashlight. If you did, douse it and light a candle when you reach the farthest, most inaccessible crack in this artery of the earth.

Now hold up the candle and see the paintings on the wall as the original artists and their guests saw them — animals leaping with pounding pulses in the flickering light of an animal-fat lamp.

These wondrous caves were discovered throughout southern Europe and, since, have become treasures of the world. Each one adds a fact to the picture of prehistoric life and helps confirm a theory or dispel a notion in the long process of uncovering the past.

And what of the scientific explorers who continued from the first accidental discoveries to uncover dozens more of these frescoed caves? Well, they had a bit of luck in their work, searching out each new cavern in the most inaccessible crack. They also had some help from their vocal apparatus.

You see, to determine which crack in the earth was best to crawl into to seek out potential paintings, they tested for acoustics. The better the acoustics, the more likely the cave held artwork. In other words, many of the prehistoric painting caverns were found by scientists singing a song.

HARMONIOUS FACT: Buddy Hassett, Brooklyn Dodgers baseball player, kept the fans in the stands during the seventh inning stretch, even when the home team was losing, by singing popular songs on the job. Professionals in all fields are making space for singing in their intense careers. The Torch Song Lawyer mixes leveraged buyouts with nightclub gigs. The Physics Chanteuse, Lynda Williams, croons familiar songs with spliced-in lyrics. "A lithium dose may cure your depression/ But carbon is a girl's best friend."

TEN WAYS TO SING AND SOLVE A PROBLEM

1. A bride and groom wanted to create unity among their guests before the wedding ceremony so they led the company in a rousing rendition of "Chapel of Love." The song and the singing turned a collection of strangers into instant community. ***Sing and create community spirit.***

2. A new counselor at Stanford Home for Children discovered an excellent way to cope with the stress of directing, interacting with, and mentoring emotionally disturbed teenagers. Each evening she sang all the way home in her car, eliminating the stress and preparing her for a good night's sleep. ***Sing and reduce stress.***

3. A substitute teacher made a great discovery after weeks of struggling with primary classroom discipline. She sang a book instead of just reading it and caught the students' rapt attention. From that day on, she used songs to focus the children and help them accomplish smooth transitions. ***Sing and work better with children.***

4. A graphic artist could not get through the interview process. She lacked the self-confidence and had trouble speaking up. She enrolled in a singing class, developed her voice, and interviewed into a job the next semester. ***Sing and get the job.***

5. A couple with a three-month-old baby found themselves facing earsplitting screaming whenever they went for a drive together; the baby hated the car seat. As they rolled down a few blocks, going deaf, the father suddenly broke out in a rousing chorus of "I've Been Working on the Railroad." The song hushed the baby and forevermore the family sang themselves into peace and quiet in the car. ***Sing and hush a baby.***

6. Guitarist Eric Clapton suffered personal tragedy when his young son died in a terrible accident. He wrote and sang his grief out in a song that became the hit, "Tears in Heaven." Many others have purged their pain after the loss of loved ones by singing. ***Sing and purge your grief.***

7. A college freshman passed a botany test by singing the facts. A junior high basketball player memorized the positions with a takeoff on "Twelve Days of Christmas." Two graduate students remembered learning Roman numerals to the tune of "Twinkle, Twinkle,

Little Star" and used it to teach the numerals to students of their own. ***Sing and learn; sing and teach.***

8. A foreman at a window factory sang "Ay Ay Cielito Lindo" whenever workers complained or grumbled. The song broke them into laughter and made it easier to solve problem situations without tempers flaring. ***Sing and keep the peace at work.***

9. Almost all businesses, schools, and organizations retire their members with a farewell dinner and speeches. At Bowling Green School, we've sent retirees off with the splendor of a song. Humorous, touching, always personal, we give our fellow workers our best with a community sing. ***Sing and toast your best with a song.***

10. I was invited to speak to a local community college crowd about my unusual (at that time) gender job of male Kindergarten teacher. After three other speakers, the crowd was ready to leave. As I approached the microphone, dozens of people stood up and began to leave. In a flash of inspiration, I broke out in a song, "Please don't stand and walk away; I have something entertaining to say." The audience laughed and sat down. ***Sing and keep your audience with you.***

Sing Away Your Fears

(Sung to "Yankee Doodle Dandy")

Sing away your fear of thunder.

Sing away your fear of death.

Sing away your claustophobia.

Sing away your fear of morning breath.

Sing away your fear of cancer.

Sing away your fear of bugs.

Sing away your fear of open spaces.

Sing away your fear of heights and thugs.

Sing away your fear of doctors.

Sing away the dentists too.

Sing away the fear of people you have never met.

Sing away your fears, you bet!

VII.
SING AND REMEMBER

Moses Supposes

In *The Prince of Egypt*, Moses is shocked by the cruelty of Pharoah. He leaves the palace and wanders in the town. Miriam and Aaron run into him. They are his sister and brother, but he does not know this truth.

Miriam begs Moses to remember his heritage. Aaron tries to keep Miriam from being executed by pretending she is crazy.

Moses does not believe—he does not want to believe—until Miriam sings a song. The song is a lullaby sung by their mother. It is a song Moses recognizes and it brings back his memory.

Miriam's singing gave Moses back his heritage and his memories. Can singing help you remember important information? Can it help you remember what must never be forgotten?

Here are some of America's folk heroes to prove it can. But first, a message from Karin Dayton, my wife...

David Francis Dayton

135

DEAR DAVID,

WHILE SHOPPING IN MEXICO WITH MY BROTHER, A SONG REALLY HELPED US OUT.

TWO YEARS EARLIER, MY DAUGHTER HAD SET THE SPANISH PHRASE "DONDE ESTA EL BANO? (WHERE IS THE BATHROOM?) TO A CATCHY TUNE TO MEMORIZE IT FOR HER SPANISH CLASS AND FOR A COUPLE OF WEEKS KEPT GOING AROUND THE HOUSE SINGING IT.

OF COURSE, WHILE IN MEXICO, THE NEED FOR THE BATHROOM AROSE.

THANKS TO REMEMBERING THE PHRASE SET TO MUSIC, I WAS ABLE TO ASK FOR THE BATH-ROOM AND THOROUGHLY IMPRESS MY BROTHER.

UNFORTUNATELY, FROM THEN ON HE EXPECTED ME TO TRANSLATE EVERYTHING.

ALTHOUGH I KNEW A LITTLE SPANISH, MY BEST SPANISH CAME FROM A SONG.

YOUR WIFE,

51. Man Versus Machine (c. 1900)

Song forbids victorious deeds to die.
—Schiller

Machines do a lot for us.

We wake to machines, prepare breakfast with machines, get to work in machines, do our work with machines, return home in machines, and relax with machines. One wonders how the world ever got along without machines.

Human labor. Muscles, brains and physical effort accomplished everything the human race needed until an invention or a machine came along to do the job better.

At one time there was a crisis between man and machine. Who was better—the man or the machine?

It could have been any machine, but in the case that mattered, it was a steam drill. It could have been any man or woman, but in the case that mattered, it was a railroad worker.

In the early 1870s, railroad laborers were building the Big Bend Tunnel on the Chesapeake and Ohio Railroad in West Virginia. The men used long-handled hammers to pound a steel drill into rock when making holes to hold blasting explosives.

Hard work. Dangerous work. And just waiting for a machine to come along to do it better.

One day, a man brought an experimental steam drill to the site. He claimed it could dig a hole faster than twenty workers using hammers. The laborers did not want a machine. It represented the industrial age and the sweat houses and the enslavement of man to machine in the frenzy of the assembly line. It also threatened to throw quite a few of them out of work. However, progress could not be halted. Unless......

The railroad laborers challenged the steam-powered drill. Perhaps it could not do what the owner claimed. Perhaps a steel-driving man could still do better.

"Fine," agreed the steam drill man. "I will pit my steam drill against any man you have."

With a unanimous shout, the railroad men called for their hero—John Henry.

The battle was drawn up. The last confrontation between man and machine as the Industrial Age broke upon the West had come. Here is one version of what happened:

They placed John Henry on the right-hand side.

The steam drill on the left. He said:

Before I let that steam drill beat me down,

I'll die with my hammer in my hand, O Lord,

And send my soul to rest.

The contest began and John slammed his hammer down as the loud scream of the steam drill rang in his ears. The laborers cheered John Henry on, and John Henry slammed his hammer down.

The truth is...John Henry won.

He laid more track than the steam-powered drill. Man triumphed over the machine. The Industrial Age stopped at the Western Frontier. John Henry paid for his triumph, however. The tunnel he labored in for his victory collapsed over his head. Yet for one moment, humanity stood tall over its own reckless achievements.

And it was all remembered in a song.

"The Ballad of John Henry" has been around one hundred years, with folk singers still singing the saga of the time when man feared machine would conquer, but it did not.

Singing the story of John Henry not only recalls to mind an individual hero, but reminds us that people still matter over technology. People still control their own destiny.

People still count—even if with a calculator.

HARMONIOUS FACT: Singing folksongs and transmitting folklore to students in school connect children to past and present cultures and enable them to participate in the history of universal human emotions.

52. I've Been Working on the Railroad (c. 1909)

And round thee with the breeze of song
To stir a little dust of praise.
—Tennyson

John Luther Jones was born in southeastern Missouri and grew to be over six feet four inches tall, with hair as dark as a locomotive engine and eyes as gray as the smoke shooting up from the stack. His Irish heart pounded with the rhythm of the wheels rolling down the track. He held but one vocation for his life.

John Luther Jones wanted to be a railroad man.

The best-known railroad jobs are those of the train crew. Most crews consist of a conductor to supervise the train's operation, an engineer to run the locomotive, one or two brakemen to uncouple cars and do various other tasks, and possibly a fireman. In the days of steam locomotives, the fireman tended the locomotive boiler.

John Luther Jones wanted to be an engineer.

He accomplished his vocation. For several years he ran freight and passengers between Jackson and Water Valley. He might have disappeared into history with the epitaph, "Engineer," and nothing more on his tombstone in Vaughan, Mississippi, except for two things: an accident and a song.

At the turn of the century, John Luther volunteered to take a sick man's place on the Cannonball Express for its southbound run from Memphis, Tennessee, to Canton, Mississippi. Joe Lewis, taken with cramps, could not take his train out. At eleven Sunday night, April 29, John Luther and his fireman, Sim Webb, climbed aboard Joe's engine number 638 and eased her out through the South Memphis yards.

At Vaughan, Mississippi, at four in the morning on April 30, two freight trains extended from a siding and blocked the main track. At fifty miles per hour, the 638 headed for an unavoidable smash-up.

"Jump, Sim, and save yourself!" ordered John Luther to his fireman. Sim jumped into some greenery along the track and escaped injury by landing on some bushes. He remembered forever the sound of the whistle screaming out a warning to the freight conductor in the caboose to jump as well.

John Luther threw the roaring locomotive into reverse and hit the air brakes, but to keep the brakes down he had to stay in the engine. The Cannonball Express crashed into the rear of the two freights, plowing through cars and caboose and rolling over on her side. Thanks to the self-sacrificing engineer holding down the brakes, 638 skidded a short distance and deaths were kept to a minimum—one. The only person killed in the crash was the engineer—John Luther.

In 1831, America's first passenger locomotive, The Best Friend of Charleston, exploded, killing the fireman—the first person in America to die in a railroad accident.

In 1833, the world's first train wreck occurred near Heightstown, New Jersey, with two deaths and many injured; two of the passengers included former President John Quincy Adams and railroad tycoon Cornelius Vanderbilt.

In 1856, two Northern Penn trains crashed head-on, slaughtering sixty-six schoolchildren bound for a picnic.

Hundreds of train disasters happened before (and hundreds worse have happened since) that day John Luther gave his life in the train crash to save the passengers and crew of the Cannonball Express. Hundreds of heroes have been briefly touted in the papers for their daring rescue work in the midst of misery and horror on the rails. Yet John Luther's story, out of all the hundreds, stays with us today.

Thanks to his friend, Wallace Saunders, a black railroad worker and songwriter.

"Wallace's admiration of Casey was little short of idolatry," said John Luther's widow during an interview in *Erie Railroad Magazine* on the twenty-eighth anniversary of his death. "He used to brag mightily about Mr. Jones, even when Casey was only a freight engineer."

Wallace always saw John Luther as a hero—a perfect subject for a song. Now, Wallace had a perfect reason for a song. He wrote up the incident in lyrics with a track-thundering melody as a tribute to his friend. Everybody loved it and everybody remembered it. An entertainer passed through town, and the railroad ballad about John Luther ended up in the act of T. Laurence Seibert and Eddie Newton, who published a rewritten version in 1909.

The published song took on a life of its own as ballads based on the song sprang up through the United States, Europe, and South Africa, and were spread by singers across three continents.

Thanks to a railroad singer, we still have the story of John Luther's heroic train ride with us today, even as trains disappear across the nation. John Luther Jones, engineer hero.

Come all you rounders for I want you to hear

The story of a brave engineer....

John Luther Jones was born in southeastern Missouri. But he was nicknamed for Cayce, Kentucky, the town where he grew up.

Casey Jones—railroad hero remembered, thanks to a railroad song.

HARMONIOUS FACT: Joe Hill, a 1914 labor activist and organizer, joined the Industrial Workers of the World and set about spreading the beliefs of the union by singing. As Joe later put it, "A pamphlet, no matter how good, is never read more than once, but a song is learned by heart and repeated over and over." Fittingly enough, Joe's memory has been kept alive by "The Ballad of Joe Hill," a song written 20 years after his death.

---

53. A Pair of Kings (c. 300)

I would rather be remembered by a song than by a victory.
—Alexander Smith

Nursery rhymes are a more enduring and endearing form of literature than are plays. They are easier to remember because they are often sung. If you want immortality, forget plays. Put your name in a nursery song.

Julius Caesar sailed across the English Channel to explore England in 55 B.C. Finding it inhabited, he returned with reinforcements a year later and trounced the native Celts before returning to Gaul. A descendant of the beleaguered British—William Shakespeare—paid homage to general Julius by putting him in a play.

Next, Emperor Claudius invaded Britannia, subdued all Celts, put down all rebellions, and kept the Scots at bay. The long line of miserable monarchs opened for business.

Local upstart Guiderius attacked the foreigner Claudius. Then Guiderius suffered betrayal during the battle and gave up the crown to Arvirargus. Arvirargus commanded the British forces, beat out Claudius' troops in a major skirmish, and cut a deal to rule as the emperor's puppet-king.

Marius came next, killing Soderic, king of the nearby Picts. Marius commemorated his hostility on a stone, then died. The crown passed to his son Coilus. He ruled in peace and prosperity. Next, Grandson Geta got the crown, but half-brother Bassianus killed him. Carausius came in with the blessing of the Roman Senate, invaded Britain, killed Bassianus. Roman legate Allectus murdered Carausius and set up in London.

Ascelpiodotus killed Allectus and promised the beseiged Romans their garrison in London would be spared if they surrendered. They surrendered, but were beheaded anyway—their heads thrown into the Nantgallum stream. Native-born King Coel defeated the Roman ursurper Ascelpiodotus. King Coel ruled in peace and prosperity.

Under Pax Romana, the Romans brought civilization to the island of Brittania. London developed as a port city.

Camps and forts, spread across the territory, became villages, towns and cities. Roman-constructed roads became the main arteries of growing commerce.

Romans raised walls to keep out the warlike Scots and other troublesome tribes. They appointed "kings" to govern the governable Celts and entrusted them with the charge to keep out the barbarians. Unfortunately, most of the monarchs ruling Brittania cared more about holding their crowns than holding back barbarians. Their violent ways resulted in violent usurpations.

As the Germanic barbarian tribes grew in power, the pressure on faraway Roman provinces increased. Brittania suffered from seafaring Angles, Saxons, and Jutes who raided, settled, and eventually conquered. Thus, Brittania became Angle-Land (England) and the majority of the people Anglo-Saxons.

For the first three hundred years of miserable monarchs in Brittania, however, two kings did give their subjects some measure of peace, prosperity, and protection from the outside barbarians. And their subjects remembered them for it.

All Brittania has remembered them for eighteen hundred years. Did you remember them—King Coilus and King Coel?

Julius Caesar—the first lord of Brittania—received a play. A portion of the literate population has seen it, possibly read it. But King Coilus and King Coel—a good pair of kings from early Brittania—received immortality through a nursery rhyme, a rhyme bearing the root of both their names.

We remember their names because we remember their song:

Old King Cole was a merry old soul and a merry old soul was he.

HARMONIOUS FACT: Good King Wenceslaus really was a king and really was good. He lived a saint and died a martyr around 989, but we remember him every Christmas, thanks to John Neale's singing verses, which plucked him from the depths of obscure history: *Good King Wenceslaus looked out on the feast of Stephen...*

54. Homer's Greatest Hits (c. 850 B.C.)

Do not commit your poems to pages alone. Sing them, I pray you.
—Virgil

Do you know the story of Troy and the Trojan Horse? Paris carried Helen off to Troy and sparked the Trojan War, a battle between Greece and present day Turkey. Famous heroes joined the battle. Even the gods took up sides.

After ten years, the Greeks won by deceit. Commander Ulysses hid his army inside a huge wooden horse and against better judgement, the Trojans took the "offering" into their fortified city. At night, Ulysses and his men poured out of the boarded bronco and slaughtered their enemies.

The indignant gods grumbled about the Greek's plywood pony. As just punishment, they caused Ulysses to sail the wrong route home. For seven years, the forsaken captain wandered the seas until finally being permitted to return to his beloved wife, Penelope.

The Trojan War, in all its glory, is preserved in a long poem called *The Iliad*. Ulysses' famous voyage home is collected in another called *The Odyssey*. Together, the two sagas, authored by Greek master poet Homer, constitute the groundwork for Western Civilization's literary heritage. Authors from medieval Dante to modernist James Joyce have paid tribute to the two epics in their own influential works. Without *The Iliad* and *The Odyssey*, Europe's cultural history might have been quite different, and much impoverished.

With those facts in mind, depart for a beach along the western coast of Greece around the year 850 B.C. ...

A blind man walks onto the beach and feels the sand blowing through his sandals and between his toes. He smiles at the crash of waves and the noise of people gathering. A booming voice directs the people to sit down, listen, be respectful. Then the man with the booming voice takes the blind man's arm and leads him to a seat of honor.

"Here is your lyre," whispers a servant and the Greek musical instrument of choice is placed into the old singer's arms.

"Tell me Muse," sang out the venerated poet as his fingers nimbly plied the strings, "of that resourceful man who was driven to wander far and wide after he had sacked the holy citadel of Troy!"

Gutenberg's printing press was still twenty-two centuries in the future.

Sheepskin scrolls consumed time and time easily comsumed them.

Homer, the renowned poet of Greek mythology, remembered and passed on the *The Iliad* and *The Odyssey*—the two landmark works of Western antiquity—by singing.

HARMONIOUS FACT: The most triumphant hero of the Greek mythmakers was not Hercules, the muscle man, but Orpheus the singer. When both joined the Argonauts to search for the Golden Fleece, Orpheus saved the entire crew (including Hercules) by outsinging the deadly Sirens. Later, Orpheus accomplished the most difficult deed in all mythology—he descended into hell, suspended damnation, and won the release of his recently departed wife. When Greek mythmakers sang the praises of the heroes, they praised most highly of their number one singer, Orpheus.

TEN WAYS TO SING AND REMEMBER

1. Rubin "Hurricane" Carter went to prison in the 1960s for a murder conviction. In 1975, Bob Dylan wrote, recorded, and released a song about his case that brought him to public attention. Not only was Carter remembered by a song, he ultimately was released due to a series of circumstances following the song. ***Sing and bring the forgotten back into the light.***

2. Charlie Maguire is the official "Singing Ranger" of the National Park Service. He sings to help others care for our natural resources. ***Put your message in a song and help others remember.***

3. Vocal groups who sing medieval and Renaissance songs experience a spiritual connection to people of those eras. ***Sing ancient songs and remember the past with emotional power.***

4. The classic education song "Mississippi" by Hanlon, Ryan, and Tierney makes spelling the state's name a snap. Apply a tune to any word you're trying to spell and the music will keep it in your head forever. ***Sing and remember how to spell.***

5. Having trouble remembering numbers? Kindergarteners can learn their phone numbers by applying the digits to the tune of "Twinkle, Twinkle, Little Star." Find a tune for that numerical information you need to recall (Social Security Number? Driver's license number?) ***Sing and remember your numbers.***

6. After the destruction of the World Trade Center Towers, all congress stood together in the aftermath and spontaneously broke out in "God Bless America!" When the nation is besieged from within or without, stand up and sing. ***Sing and remember your patriotism.***

7. A gentleman at his father's funeral heard the choir break forth in Handel's "Hallelujah Chorus." He was in no mood to hear it, even sung by friends. But as the choir sang, he discovered his body straightening, his mouth opening, and with an explosion of sudden joy he joined in. He sang and was drawn out of his grief and isolation, back into relation with God and his community. ***Sing and remember your faith.***

8. The German-American club gets together to remember their heritage, celebrate old customs, and sing. The Filipino-Americans pass on their traditions and culture through singing of the Passion during Lent. Hundreds of groups across America remember their past and pass it along to their children through religion, recipes, and songs. ***Sing and remember your cultural heritage.***

9. The abolitionists did it with "John Brown's Body." Singer Stonewall Jackson did it with "Waterloo." Jimmy Dean did it with "P.T. 109." Dion did it with "Abraham, Martin, and John." George Harrison did it with "When We Was Fab." Most recently, Bruce Springsteen did it with his album *The Rising*, an artistic response to the World Trade Center tragedy. Hundreds of songwriters have eulogized people, places, and events. ***Sing and remember the past.***

10. Turn on those "oldies" radio stations and sing along. Turn on your memory and hum the tunes you heard around the house from your father, your mother, your grandparents. And especially recall the songs you sang with your friends. ***Sing and remember your past.***

Sing to Remember

(Sung to "My Bonnie Lies Over the Ocean")

Sing to remember your history.
Sing to remember the past.
Sing to make some small connection
To people of yore that will last.
Sing to remember
Sing to remember your heritage.
Sing to remember
Sing to remember it all.

David Francis Dayton

VIII.
SING AND SEE THE INCREDIBLE

The Singing Lion

In *The Magician's Nephew*, one of the Narnian Chronicles by C.S. Lewis, a boy, a girl, a cabby, a witch, and a magician find themselves standing in black and empty space where nothing is. It is one moment before the act of creation.

How does creation begin? With a song.

A great lion—a lion called Aslan—begins to sing, and when he sings, realities come into being. Mountains take shape, trees grow, animals appear. The world of Narnia explodes into life through singing.

Can singing make a world out of nothing?

Can singing make us see the incredible?

President William Henry Harrison, cowboy singer Gene Autry, Beatle George Harrison and others will show us it can.

Catherine Dayton

55. Clearing a Confederate's Name (c. 1868)

And now I am their song, yea, I am their byword.
—Job 30:09

The music industry is a marvelous institution. Barefoot poets in rags plunk guitars, get recorded, and become overnight millionaires. In the Beatles' hometown of Liverpool—in the early 1960s—recording companies emptied the neighborhoods of skiffle bands (any quartet of teenagers with cheap instruments) in a mad dash to capture the next money-making sound or the next electrifying group.

Not all beneficiaries of the music industry are barefoot poets, however. Some are barefoot soldiers.

Being an ex-soldier after any war is hard. Being an ex-soldier after an unpopular war is harder. Being an ex-Confederate soldier must have been concrete. Tom Dula, a 22-year-old Confederate veteran of Company K, Forty-Second Regiment, walked onto Major James W. M. Grayson's farm at Trade, Tennessee, during the summer after the Civil War and begged for employment. His shoes were worn out and he needed money for boots. He said he came from Wilkes County, North Carolina.

The Major gave the veteran four days of work, enough to buy the boots. Tom Dula left early on the fifth day, wearing the boots. Late that afternoon, deputies from Wilkes County, North Carolina, arrived.

The deputies told the Major that veteran Tom Dula was wanted for murder. They shared details about jealous lovers and the gruesome knife slaying of a young girl. Shocked, the Major extended his hospitality to the deputies for the night and promised to track down the accused in the morning.

On July 11, 1866, Major Grayson buckled on his seven shot rimfire Deemore .32 caliber revolver and led the deputies forth. Tom Dula stood barefoot in Doe Creek, soaking the blisters rubbed up by his new boots. Caught shoeless, footsore, and without a gun, Dula gave up.

The deputies—hot for justice—hankered for lynching Dula on the spot in Tennessee. The Major wanted no blood shed in Tennessee. Furthermore, he had had his fill of illegal hangings during the war. He raised his Deemore .32 caliber revolver and convinced the deputies to deliver the accused whole and living to a fair trial. The troop marched back to the Major's farm.

The following morning, Major Grayson tied Tom Dula's hands, then roped Dula's feet underneath the belly of the horse and set out to deliver the prisoner to Wilkes County Jail in North Carolina.

Though the state failed to produce a murder victim during Dula's imprisonment, and committed several errors attendant to the arrest and confinement of Tom Dula, the Confederate veteran was hanged at Statesville, North Carolina, on May 1, 1868, for the murder and secret burial of 21-year-old Laura Foster. Ann Melton—the "other woman"—was also charged. But Tom Dula claimed full responsibility for the crime on the eve of his hanging. His confession set Ann Melton free.

Tom Dula and his murder trial would have faded into turn-of-the-century history except for one thing—a song. Some believe Tom Dula composed the song himself. There is a fanciful story of his walk to the gallows, singing verses in his Southern baritone and playing the tune on his fiddle. Some prisoners ask for a last meal; some say Tom Dula asked to play a last melody.

However it came about, the song took on a longer life than Tom Dula and spread among the mountain folk who sympathized with the soldier's plight. Several versions appeared as the tune became a standard in the Great Smokies.

Major Grayson's nephew, Gilliam Banmon Grayson of Laurel Bloomery, Tennessee, took one version and made the first recording of the work for Victor Records on October 1, 1929. The first Grayson had wanted Dula to get a fair trial; the next generation Grayson wanted Dula's dirge to get a fair hearing.

The song grew in stature in 1938, when folksinger-collector Frank Warner heard it from Frank Proffitt, a young mountaineer from Pick Britches Valley, North Carolina. Warner passed it along to Alan Lomax who published a version in his influential folk anthology, *Folk Song USA*.

Then, in 1957, a wandering singer carried the weathered "classic" to the Purple Onion nightclub. The fellow sang the song with a major change. Instead of "Tom Dula" he called the Confederate soldier "Tom Dooley."

The management sent the unknown singer away—probably back to the hills of Tennessee—but the song caught the ears of three employed singers at the club. They called themselves The Kingston Trio and the song by the unknown singer sounded perfect for their first album. Capitol Records released the album.

Two disc jockeys in Salt Lake City (Confederates at heart?) played the ballad all day long and recommended the record to other markets. Demand for "Tom Dooley" compelled Capitol Records to issue a single.

The rapid and far-reaching success of "Tom Dooley" and the Kingston Trio revolutionized popular music. Folk music found a following and set the stage for such artists as Bob Dylan, Joan Baez, and Peter, Paul, and Mary. All good and well for Capitol Records, but what about our Confederate soldier?

Well, Tom Dula was right to ask for a last song instead of a last meal. The ballad of his life sold over three million copies. And when the Kingston Trio release reached number one on the charts, North Carolina took action.

Tom Dula's ignored and abandoned grave received a public restoration. Tom Dula received a posthumous pardon.

The music industry is a marvelous institution. It can take a barefoot poet and turn him into a millionaire. It can take a barefoot soldier and wipe his history clean.

Tom Dula—ex-confederate of the Civil War—cleared of murder and his name saved from disgrace—by a song.

HARMONIOUS FACT: American folk songwriter Stephen Foster made sure his wife would live forever by putting her into a song: "I Dream of Jeanie With the Light Brown Hair."

---

56. General Frances E. Willard (c. 1840)

A bird does not sing because it has an answer.
It sings because it has a song.
—Chinese Proverb

Frances E. Willard was a feminist.

Frances E. Willard was a women's rights activist.

Frances E. Willard was a mover and a shaker of the '90s.

The 1890s.

While other girls were playing with dolls, Frances was imbibing lectures on the evils of liquor. While other girls were going to fancy balls, Frances was taking notes on suffragettes. While other girls were getting married, Frances was getting an education.

She earned a college degree, taught at a seminary, and associated with Dwight Moody in the evangelist movement. The National Women's Temperance Union elected her president in 1879.

She organized the Prohibition Party in 1882 and, in 1883, founded and served as president of the Women's Christian Temperance Union, a world-wide organization, laying the groundwork for what would later become the passage of the Prohibition Amendment.

When the Congress called to hear Frances speak, Susan B. Anthony introduced Miss Willard as a "general with an army of 250,000."

When the Congress called for statues of two prominent citizens from each state to place in Statuary Hall in the Capitol, Illinois sent two generals: James Shield from the War Between the States and Frances Willard from the War on Alcohol.

Many testify to Frances E. Willard's considerable skills as an orator and speaker, as an educator and reformer. She pioneered in the temperance movement and organized its efforts in such a way that the movement gained national attention. She never saw it, but her achievements changed the Constitution twice over.

How does a child develop the zeal for such a vocation? How did a girl develop such a zeal in the 1840s when expectations for women ran nowhere near the political arena, let alone reworking the federal government of the United States?

Frances E. Willard's zeal and drive went back to one Sunday evening when her father, farmer Willard, taught his little girl the hymn, "A Charge To Keep I Have."

To serve the present age

My calling to fulfill

Oh may it all my powers engage

To do my Master's will!

Farmer Willard told his daughter the song meant that God brought her into the world to fulfill that verse. He told Frances she had a destiny and a purpose. Together they sang the hymn and the message imprinted itself upon the girl's heart.

Frances would be somebody.

Frances would accomplish something.

She did.

And today a statue of Frances stands in Statuary Hall. She was the first woman to be so honored.

Thanks to zeal...a father...and a song.

HARMONIOUS FACT: In 1957, Ethel Waters walked into Madison Square Garden to attend one of the Billy Graham Crusades and she "felt that my Lord was calling me back home." Asked to sing a solo, she sang, "His Eye Is on the Sparrow." For five nights at the crusade, Ethel Waters sang that song. The experience changed her life. She testified, "I found that I could no longer act every role I was offered and continue to glorify my Lord." Singing gave her a new vision for her life.

---

57. Coffin Clocks (c. 1875)

At what I sing there's some may smile,
While some, perhaps, will sigh.
—Thomas More

And now a word about coffins.

Coffins begin with the flat lid variety. Then comes the single raised lid. Gold etching follows. Fancy interior is next. I suppose you could line up expensive coffins until you reached all the way to King Tut's body-shaped funeral box. His coffin boasted solid gold.

Coffins are not the kind of thing one keeps about the house, unless it is a house of the dead. Coffins are neither strong enough nor comfortable enough to sit on. Coffins do not make good toy chests. And coffins do have the unfortunate connotations of the funeral home. Say *coffin* and the average person thinks of death.

Would you move into a coffin house?

Would you buy a coffin car?

Would you sleep in a coffin bed?

What does all this coffin business have to do with anything? Well, coffins do have a close affinity to dead people. In England, a man died and, though he certainly found his way to a coffin, it was the coffin he left behind that inspired an American songwriter to change one small part of history, forever.

Henry Work wrote songs for a living. He did passably well. Then he took a trip to England and stayed at the George Hotel where he heard a story that fascinated him.

A man died and his clock stopped forever at the moment of his death.

Henry rushed back to America with lyrics and a song about the amazing clock that timed its own demise with that of its owner. The song sold over a million copies of sheet music and made a few changes in Henry's life.

Oh my grandfather's clock was too tall for the shelf

so it stood ninety years on the floor.

It was taller by half than the old man himself,

though it weighed not a pennyweight more....

You might know the song. You may know the grandfather clock. Did you ever consider what the song did for the clock? Naturally, a hit song is going to spread the news.

Grandfather clocks make a house into a home.

Grandfather clocks make a family heirloom.

Grandfather clocks are good business.

Singing the song no doubt increased the desire for grandfather clocks. Singing the song no doubt spread the name and popularity of grandfather clocks. But one fact has yet to be elaborated. Would you buy a coffin car, a coffin lamp, a coffin desk? Probably not. And you probably would not have had much interest in a coffin clock.

Until coffin clocks changed their name to grandfather clocks...thanks to a public singing a song.

HARMONIOUS FACT: In 1954, the popular song "Three Coins in the Fountain" turned the Fountain of Trevi in Italy into a major tourist attraction.

---

58. The Titanic and Other Disasters (c. 1912)

A good song is none the worse for being sung twice.
—Tennyson

How do people cope with disaster?

When the Civil War began in 1861, the first man in the town of Poland to volunteer for the army was McKinley. At the Battle of Antietam, the man who brought food to his regiment despite intense enemy assault was McKinley. Bravery under fire earned McKinley a promotion. During his later political career, folks would call him Major McKinley. Then, President McKinley.

As President, McKinley faced a crisis with Spain over Cuba. In 1895, Cubans began a rebellion against Spain, which had ruled Cuba for almost four hundred years.   After McKinley took office in 1897, he pressed Spain to negotiate with the rebels. The President wanted to remain neutral in the affair.   However, McKinley said that the United States would go to war if necessary to protect U.S. interests.

The battleship U.S.S. Maine exploded in Havana harbor in Cuba. The public blamed Spain for the sinking. Under extreme pressure from politicians, newspaper publishers, and the loud public, McKinley asked Congress for authority to take action. On April 25, the United States declared war on Spain. The U.S. Army and Navy overpowered the Spanish forces and under the agreement of the Treaty of Paris, the war came to an end.

McKinley's troubles did not.

On September 6, the President held a reception in the Pan American Exposition's Temple of Music. A handkerchief covered the revolver that anarchist Leon F. Czolgosz carried in his right hand. When the President approached him to shake hands, Czolgosz fired two bullets at McKinley. One bullet richocheted off his button, but the other pierced his stomach. Eight days later, overwhelmed by gangrene and infection, McKinley died.

Another disaster of a different kind struck in 1912.

Another ship sank. This ship did not start a war, but it did lose fifteen hundred passengers and crew, more than half its original 2,200. Unlike McKinley, this ship sailed out looking for disaster. It stuck out a haughty chin at fate, calling itself the "unsinkable." It carried only enough lifeboats for about half its human cargo. Who needs lifeboats when a boat is unsinkable? It cruised along at top speed in dangerous waters when it should have been going much slower because of the natural obstacles appearing in the water all around.

In 1912, the Titanic, a British passenger ship, struck an iceberg and sank in the North Atlantic Ocean on the liner's first voyage. It sideswiped the iceberg at about 11:40 p.m. on April 14. The impact caused a number of small cracks and failed riveted seams in the ship's hull. Seawater flooded through the bow of the ship. Two and a half hours later, the vessel broke in two and sank.

Disaster comes at many times and in many places. McKinley knew he was going to die just as the Titanic passengers knew they were going to sink. But how did they face those disasters?

The same way.

As the band on the Titanic played on to the end, the passengers left aboard gathered and sang. Bandleader Wallace Hartley held one song in particular as his favorite. He often expressed the wish that it be performed at his funeral. Apparently, it was.

And as McKinley felt the last of his strength ebbing away on the hospital bed, he whispered the first verse to that same song. President, bandleader, and passengers met death with the same hymn. They sang, "Nearer My God to Thee," to meet death.

HARMONIOUS FACT: Geoffrey O' Hara wrote the hymn, "There Is No Death," and shares the story of a singer whose dead mother appears as he sings this song. Ever since writing it, he has been hearing from people who had either lost their fear of death after listening to the song, or had felt a similar contact with a departed loved one. Sing and meet death with less fear.

59. The Governor Who Wrote a Song (c. 1941)

*It is the best means to procure a perfect pronounciation,
and to make a good Orator.*
—William Byrd.

Songs can take us to faraway places. Songs can take us to emotional heights. Songs can take us to Capitol Hill.

Ask Pappy O' Daniels.

When Congress debated the twenty-second amendment which imposed term limits on presidents, W. Lee "Pass the Biscuits, Pappy" O'Daniels proposed limits for all elective officials. Careerism is the dominant motive of most legislators. Term limits would make members of Congress servants of the Republic rather than followers of public opinion.

However, Congress decided not to follow up on Pappy's idea. His novel proposal (which might have redefined American politics) lost eighty-two to one. Such is one of Pappy's claims to fame.

Pappy became a U.S. senator in 1941. He did it by defeating Lyndon Johnson, a future president. Such is another of Pappy's claims to fame.

But Pappy's first claim to fame—before Johnson and before his term limits proposal—was a band and a song. In fact, his song made all his other amazing feats possible.

Pappy O' Daniels sat on the board of directors for Burris Mills Flours. Not an exciting job. But Pappy conceived an exciting idea. He decided that sales of Burris Mills Flours might increase if the right kind of publicity could be generated over the radio. He formed a band—"The Light Crust Doughboys"—and placed them on local station KFJZ.

Milton Brown's vocalizing made the band a success. Pappy's bet about publicity paid off. Burris Flour sales increased. Now Pappy wanted to take advantage of the publicity. He moved the band from KFJZ to KTAT where he secured the band's announcer job for himself. Now the audience heard Milton's Brown's vocalizing, the band's music, and Pappy O'Daniels's voice. The admiration of the public for the band rubbed off onto Pappy through association.

The band members did not share the public's admiration for Pappy. He paid them salaries below the poverty line. When Milton Brown asked Pappy for a raise, Milton did not get it. So Milton left to form a competitive band back on the original station KFJZ.

Pappy brought in singer Tommy Duncan, altered the band's style, and kept plugging on the radio, pumping up his image as the entrepreneur who really cared for the common man. Now Pappy felt the time had come for him to take his publicity stunt to the next level.

Although he used the band first to sell flour, and second to sell himself, Pappy really did appreciate music. He learned to sing and he learned to write songs. His most popular song was "The Boy Who Never Grew Too Old to Comb His Mother's Hair." Once he figured out how best to croon it, he crooned it all across Texas.

He crooned it at meetings and assemblies. He crooned it at picnics and barbecues. He crooned it in parades and over the airwaves and just about anywhere he could find a voting American.

Americans like songs. Songs can take us to faraway places and emotional heights. Songs can even make people vote for us.

Ask Pappy O' Daniels—the first proponent of term limits.

Ask Pappy O'Daniels—the man who defeated Lyndon Johnson.

Ask Pappy O' Daniels—the first American politician to sing his way into the governorship of Texas (and thence on to Capitol Hill)—with a song.

HARMONIOUS FACT: James Houston Davis bought and sang "You Are My Sunshine" in a successful campaign to the Texas governor's mansion, an encore performance of the Pappy O' Daniels triumph in Austin.

---

60. A Sometimes Man (c. 1836)

He ceased. But still their trembling ears retained
The deep vibrations of his witching song.
—James Thomson

William Henry Harrison was a sometimes man. Sometimes he won. Sometimes he lost. He tried to study medicine and lost. He joined the army and won.

He governed over the Indians' welfare and successfully inoculated them against smallpox. Then he negotiated a treaty with the Indian leaders that was later denounced and started a war.

Harrison fought and won a brilliant victory over combined Indian and British forces in the Battle of the Thames in southern Ontario. He quarreled with the secretary of war and lost, resigning from the army.

He won election to the United States House of Representatives. Then he was accused of misusing public money. He accepted an appointment as the U.S. minister to Colombia, but his blunt tongue caused him to be replaced within a year. He ran for President and lost.

Enough of this winning and losing, decided William and his supporters. From now on they were only going to win. Out with the old line of debates and politicking. The next election would find them employing a more effective means of running a political race.

William and his supporters sat down and wrote a song. For a catchy title, they reached back to General William Henry Harrison's victory over the Indians at present-day Lafayette during the Battle of Tippecanoe whence he earned the nickname, "Tippecanoe." They added in the alliterative running mate Tyler and soon had a song that would roll off everybody's lips.

Oh! Who has heard the great commotion,

Motion, motion

All the country through?

It is the ball a rollin' on

For Tippecanoe and Tyler too,

For Tippecanoe and Tyler too.

Another verse took pot shots at the opponent—Martin Van Buren.

And with them we'll beat little Van.

Van, Van, Van is a used up man.

The political machine did not stop with one big hit. The Harrison camp employed dozens of writers and put out dozens of songs. One of his most successful songsters was the future newspaper editor, Horace Greeley. He started *Log Cabin*, a campaign paper dedicated to the propagation of song lyrics in favor of Harrison. He penned and printed the lyrics and gave the public popular melodies to hang the songs upon.

At 80,000 copies a week, the paper flooded the Union with musical propaganda, encouraging Greeley to note, "Our songs are doing more good than anything else." The music became so renowned that groups such as the "Tippecanoe Glee Club" and the "Tippecanoe Boys" kicked off rallies with their renditions of the Log Cabin songs in what has been called "the most singingest campaign in U.S. history."

What Harrison was unable to do with plain politics, he accomplished easily with a folio of refrains and one big hit song. The country voted the song character and his mate Tyler into the White House over Martin Van Buren in 1836.

Despite his assistance from singing, Harrison followed his usual pattern of win-lose. After thirty days in office, he caught a bad cold, developed pneumonia, and died.

William Henry Harrison—the sometimes man—whose life teaches the excellent lesson that politicians who can inspire their supporters to sing sometimes get elected.

HARMONIOUS FACT: Blues composer W.C. Handy wrote "Mr. Crump" (later retitled, "Memphis Blues") to promote E.H. Crump, a reform candidate running for the office of mayor in Memphis, Tennessee. The song attracted an overwhelming number of voters to the polls for Crump and contributed to his victory.

61. Cowboy on a Reindeer (c. 1949)

What fun it is to ride and sing a sleighing song tonight!
—James Pierpont

Traditions usually come first and songs follow afterwards. The season of Christmas used to stretch from Christmas Day until January 12th, resulting in the well-known carol, "The Twelve Days of Christmas." Another thousand songs grew from the events of the Nativity—"Silent Night," "Away in a Manger," "O Little Town of Bethlehem," and so on. The events came first, then the songs.

But once upon a time, a Christmas song came first, and helped generate the legend afterwards. To accomplish this feat required three dissimilar elements: a cowboy, a department store, and a brother-in-law.

The cowboy was Gene Autry, who sang his way to fame in the movies from the 1930s through the early 1950s. Not only did he sing, he also wrote hits such as "Tears on My Pillow" (1941) and added another song to Christmas with "Here Comes Santa Claus" (1947). Then, in 1949, Autry recorded his greatest success, not by singing on the back of a horse, but by singing backup to a deer.

The deer came from the Montgomery Ward department store. They asked their copywriter, Robert L. May, to come up with a Christmas story to give away to customers as a promotional gimmick. Their initial reason was merely to save money; they never expected to initiate a myth. Mr. May played around with an idea about an underdog reindeer and tested it on his four-year-old daughter. She loved the story so the department store gave the project a go-ahead.

The book broke forth one Yuletide season with moderate success. The printed version of the underdog reindeer fulfilled its obligations of saving money. It even began to make money. True legend-making boiled over in the pot when the copyright ownership fell into the hands of the copywriter. Once debt-ridden May owned the rights to his underdog reindeer, he turned in haste to his talented brother-in-law—songwriter Johnny Marks.

Brother-in-law Marks transformed the original story into a set of lyrics with a catchy melody. Unfortunately, few wanted to record it. This upstart reindeer tampered with the traditions of a popular holiday.

Enter the cowboy.

Imagine a cowboy singing a song about a Christmas reindeer! At least it could have been a horse. Gene Autry almost turned it down as well, but didn't. Gene Autry, the good guy singing cowboy, retained his hero image and saved the reindeer from oblivion.

"Rudolph the Red-Nosed Reindeer" exploded upon the world in Christmas of 1949 and sold two million copies. Department store copywriter Robert L. May paid his wife's doctor bills. Talented brother-in-law Johnny Marks expanded his success by writing the score to the Rudolph television special. And singing cowboy Gene Autry became a successful business executive and owner of the California Angels baseball team. Rudolph fully established himself as part of Christmas folklore, thanks to a department store's concept, a brother-in-law's lyrical skills, and a cowboy singing his song.

Over the years, Rudolph and Gene established themselves in record-selling history with 50 million copies—the best-selling record of all time after Bing Crosby's "White Christmas."

HARMONIOUS FACT: Traditions can be made or broken with singing. Mae Bertha Carter's children were the first to integrate their Mississippi school in the 1960s, breaking a long-standing tradition in the Southern school system. How did she face the fears and problems resulting from her daring decision? She drew inspiration from singing.

---

62. Million Seller Lesson Plans (c. 1959)

What will a child learn sooner than a song?
—Alexander Pope

Did you ever hear about the teacher whose lesson plan sold over a million copies? The subject of his lesson was Andrew Jackson.

Andrew Jackson waited for the British with his wild mix of troops in New Orleans. Regular Army units, dandy New Orleans militia, a contingent of former Haitian slaves fighting as free men, Kentucky and Tennessee frontiersmen, and a colorful band of outlaws used dirt, cotton bales, and sugar barrels to build a strong barricade against the British who invaded the city on January 8, 1815.

As usual, the British soldiers made perfect targets as they marched across open ground and fell by the dozens. The Americans killed or wounded two thousand British and captured hundreds more, giving His Majesty's army their biggest defeat in the entire war. The American loss amounted to twenty-two killed or wounded.

Thanks to the victory, General Andrew Jackson became a national hero and later our seventh president. A sense of national pride sprang up from the Battle of New Orleans, the last battle of the war.

Now, with the subject of the lesson firmly established, let us move ahead twelve decades to find our teacher in rural Arkansas during the economic slump of the Great Depression. James Morris tackled education in those depressed times. At twenty-nine, he worked hard as a dedicated teacher, but could not get students interested in learning history—until he tried singing.

Morris came from a family of singers, so he hit on the idea of writing poems about historic events and setting them to music. The scheme worked. Students began to pay attention to something they formerly showed no interest in.

One of Jimmy's compositions used a fiddle tune known as "The Eighth of January" that celebrated the Andrew Jackson victory. Jimmy wrote up the historic fight as "The Battle of New Orleans" and it helped explain to his high school students that the Battle of New Orleans happened during the War of 1812 instead of during the Revolutionary War.

Over the years Jimmy "Driftwood," as he came to be known, brought his songs with him to other schools where he taught, developing a reputation across the region's school districts in towns such as Snowball, Timbo, and Mountain View.

Although designed only as teaching tools, the song about Andrew Jackson caught the interested ear of country recording star Jimmy Horton who recorded "The Battle of New Orleans." It became the smash hit of 1959, selling more than a million copies, and eventually wound up on a list of the "Ten Most Popular American Songs of All Time."

Educator Jimmy Driftwood would go on to receive an Honorary Doctorate Degree in Folklore from Peabody University in Nashville. Singer Jimmy Driftwood would go on to compose over six thousand songs, lay claim to several chart hits ("The Tennessee Stud," "Down in the Arkansas," "He Had a Long Chain On"), and receive two Grammy Awards.

But it all started with a teacher who believed he could improve his teaching with a song—a million dollar lesson-plan song.

HARMONIOUS FACT: Singing in school has many benefits. Kindergarten students have learned their phone numbers by singing the digits to the tune of "Twinkle, Twinkle, Little Star," and elementary and high school students have memorized key facts by "piggybacking" the words onto popular song lyrics.

---

63. The Two Worlds of George Harrison (c. 1971)

It seems to me I've heard that song before.
—Jule Styne

As one of the Fab Four, Beatle George Harrison sang in the sixties to help create a subculture, give voice to protest, and direct a generation. But all by himself, George Harrison managed to change two worlds with his songs.

First, in 1971, George released a solo album after the Beatles broke up, entitled *All Things Must Pass*. On that album George sang a song destined to make history.

"My Sweet Lord" sold well, but a few years later someone wanted some of the money. Apparently, George had unconsciously borrowed the melody for "My Sweet Lord" from an earlier popular song, "He's So Fine."

Ronnie Mack, the writer of "He's So Fine," died the day his song made number one. He would not be around to hear George's rewrite on his old tune. But the inheritors of Ronnie Mack's estate, or better, the inheritors of the estate which included "He's So Fine," did hear it and immediately put their lawyers on the case to see whether or not "My Sweet Lord" would pay up.

The legal battle made history, with George in the courtroom playing his guitar, and the case is now a classic for study by lawyers around the country and over the world.

George may have gotten stung by his inadvertant use of an old melody, but he contributed to the advancement of law through his singing.

Sing and give others an education in law.

Sing and change the legal world.

Sing and change the fate of the world.

George Harrison answered the call when his friend, Ravi Shankar, asked him for advice about putting together a benefit performance for the hungry and ravaged people of the recently established country of Bangladesh. Ravi thought realistically: Raise $25,000 and feed starving people. George thought big: Get some famous friends together and put on a concert like no other.

Flanked by Eric Clapton and old Beatle buddy Ringo Starr, George put on the rock concert of the century with a surprise appearance by Bob Dylan. The Internal Revenue Service stumbled in to drag out the distribution of funds, but the benefit performance eventually raised nine million dollars and went on to change the world as Harrison's model of generosity inspired other rock stars to follow.

In 1979, George's fellow ex-Beatle, Paul McCartney, collected some English rock and rollers to raise several million dollars for starving refugees from Kampuchea, caught in the fighting in Vietnam and Cambodia.

In 1984, Bob Geldof collected three dozen musicians to record "Do They Know It's Christmas? (Feed the World)" to raise millions for Ethiopian famine relief.

In 1985, singer Harry Belafonte drew inspiration from the Geldof effort to organize the biggest collection of singer stars ever assembled to put out "We Are the World," a music video superseller written by Lionel Ritchie and Michael Jackson. "We Are the World" became the classic model of the now-popular singing benefit as musicians from the entire range of popular music joined in a chorus to raise a staggering $50 million.

But it all started with George Harrison and his idea to change the fate of one part of the world by singing a song.

HARMONIOUS FACT: Not to be outdone by "We Are the World," Bob Geldof went on to develop a novel approach in the singing benefit with a pair of Live Aid concerts in Philadelphia and London. Broadcast in 155 countries around the world, these well-planned works raised $144 million to fight world hunger.

---

64. The Kansas Rocking Bird (c. 1966)

*Use what talents you possess; the woods would be very silent
if no birds sang there except those that sang best.*
—Henry Jackson Vandyke Jr.

Do you think you lack a beautiful voice?

Do you think your tone is just a bit off?

Well, chances are, no one has ever complained that your voice has the quality of "cockroaches dancing in a trashcan." That is what people said about Mrs. Elva Miller. Mrs. Elva Miller wanted to be a singer. She practiced with the high school glee club. The glee club responded without glee. She sang with her church choir. The choir considered her contribution less than heavenly. She took classes and studied voice at Pomona College in Claremont, California. The teacher should have flunked her.

But Elva Miller's determination to sing and be a success overcame all the obstacles. Maybe she could not sing well, but she could and would sing.

She recorded her own version of "Downtown," a song made famous by Petula Clark, and somehow persuaded a local DJ to send out over the airwaves what many critics would later call a "nightmarish" single.

No doubt the DJ thought he was having a bit of fun with Elva and the listening public as well. He never reckoned on the power of positive singing. In three weeks, the crazy recording of "Downtown" with the musical quality of "cockroaches in a trashcan" sold over 250,000 copies. Mrs. Elva Miller became known as the "Kansas Rocking Bird," a sudden sensation and talk show guest. With subsequent record releases, she rose to the rank of a national figure, appearing on the *Ed Sullivan Show*, among others.

At fifty-nine, the childless, plumpish housewife from the Los Angeles suburb of Claremont made a movie, *The Cool Ones*, with Roddy McDowall, and traveled to Vietnam to entertain the troops. She gave superstar concerts to adoring fans and on occasion visited terminally ill children to uplift them with not-quite-right versions of popular songs, including "A Hard Day's Night" by the Beatles.

All these accomplishments thanks to singing.

Bad singing.

You can still find Elva's contributions to discography. Here is a sample of what is available in the collector's market:

Mrs. Miller's Greatest Hits (LP), 1969, Capitol

Will Success Spoil Mrs. Miller? (LP), Capitol

The Country Soul Of Mrs. Miller (LP), Capitol

You can also find a Mrs. Miller Christmas album, and, of course, the original hit—"Downtown/A Lover's Concerto."

Mrs. Miller changed her life and millions of others by singing. Even though her voice sounded like "cockroaches in a trash can."

HARMONIOUS FACT: Florence Foster Jenkins spent thirty years singing for the public in spite of a voice critics called "preposterous, filled with squawks and quavers." She could not carry a tune. Yet she gathered admirers—among them Enrico Caruso—for her bravura and the sheer entertainment she provided with her uncertain rhythm and "sliding scale" sense of melody. In 1944, in a climax to an outlandish and incredible singing career, Florence Foster Jenkins sang in a sold-out performance at Carnegie Hall in New York.

TEN WAYS TO SING AND SEE THE INCREDIBLE

1. A three-year-old girl fell off her tricycle and smashed her upper lip. One of the teeth turned black, signaling the death of the nerve. Her parents—Christian Scientists—prayed and sang songs of healing for her. Within a few days, the tooth regained its color; they took her to a dentist, not for treatment, but merely to verify the health of her teeth. All was well. *Sing and see incredible healing.*

2. A retired colonel liked to sing and play harmonica for patients in the local hospital. One day, he played "Amazing Grace" for a bedridden woman. Lying next to her was a lady who had been comatose for two years. In the middle of the song, he thought he saw the comatose woman wink. He walked over and asked if she would like to hear "Just a Closer Walk with Thee." She opened her eyes

and smiled through the whole song. When he finished, she went back to sleep. *Sing and awaken the forever sleeping.*

3. Several college students arrived in Paris after spending the day being jostled on trains, lost on streets, and hungry for lack of access to the language. They saw Notre Dame cathedral and entered in time for the mass. Here is their own account: "We took off our heavy packs and began to relax..the opening song filled the cathedral and immediately put us at ease...we looked around and saw a mixture of tourists and civilians, singing in all different languages the processional song "Ave Maria." My friend and I began singing in English, as the French and Latin tongues intertwined together...all different languages, singing the same song as one....I finally felt comfortable and at peace...one song connected us all as one joined congregation in that Mass. We felt a little more at home, all through the singing of a shared song." *Sing and find community away from home.*

4. When a group of charities asked German-born musician Handel to orchestrate a new work to benefit the needy, the great composer set about writing his most famous work. When he finished the Hallelujah Chorus, he said, "I did think I did see all Heaven before me, and the great God himself." The money raised released 142 men from debtor's prison and secured Handel's success. *Sing and see fortunes reversed.*

5. Donnie Osmond joined his brothers on a trip to Disneyland. Dressed alike, they caught the eye of the Dapper Dans, a professional barber shop quartet performing on Main Street. The quartet asked the boys if they could sing in harmony. The brothers promptly did. The performance led to a contract with Disneyland where they were discovered by Jay Williams who told his son Andy to book them for his show. *Sing and be discovered, even on vacation.*

6. A taxi driver feared for his job after an unfortunate collision on the streets of Pennsylvania in 1943. His passenger—an upper class heiress—had been irrevocably changed by the accident. However, his fare was the renowned "world's worst opera singer," Florence Foster Jenkins. The "damage" from the accident made her capable of warbling a higher F than she'd ever managed before. Delighted with the "side effects" of the collision, she waived legal action, and gave the cab driver a gift box of imported cigars. Her improved ability to sing saved the driver's career and helped her own. *Sing and forgive serious injuries.*

7. Spike Jones and his madcap troupe performed a song during World War II entitled "Der Fuehrer's Face," a mockery of Hitler and the Nazis. The tune was written and performed for a Disney cartoon and became a last-minute choice to fill the second side of a record. The song's amazing success established Spike Jones and his band for the first time and renamed the cartoon. *Sing and see incredible success.*

8. The Bobbettes wrote an unflattering song about their teacher, Mr. Lee, whom they disliked immensely. But when they were signed to record for Atlantic, the music executives revised the lyrics to make the song less controversial and more commericial. The song "Mr. Lee" went Top Ten in July, 1957, making Mr. Lee—the despised instructor—the best known and beloved teacher in America. *Sing and see life go topsy-turvey.*

9. Aura Lee, Annie Laurie, Donna, Linda, and a thousand other women have been immortalized in a song. Once upon a time they lived and once upon a time they died. But thanks to a song, a song people keep singing, their names stay alive forevermore. *Sing and immortalize someone you love.*

10. Shipwreck victims off the Falklands survived seven days without food, rowing two hundred miles on the strength of an inspiring hymn. Emily Beck donned a life jacket and plunged into the sea when her ship caught fire. Near unconsciousness and numbed by the cold, she sang a hymn to keep awake until she was finally rescued. Hundreds of accounts exist of people hanging on to life in dire circumstances thanks to a devotional song. *Sing and hang in there.*

Sing to See a Miracle

(Sung to "God Bless America")

Sing to see a miracle.
Sing to praise your God.
Sing to cast out
All demons.
Sing to lift up this life we must trod.

Sing to find faith.
Sing to find hope.
Sing to find love and charity.
Sing to see a miracle.
Sing out as on you trod.
Sing to attune the mind
And soul to God.

IX.
A SONG TO GET YOU STARTED

Author's Solo

*One of the obligations of the writer
is to say or sing all that he or she can...*
—Denise Levertov

Have you ever sung a song and saved your life? I'm no professional singer, but I like to sing, and have used singing for many good purposes: worshiping God, celebrating family events, and preventing death—my own.

Research shows that the act of singing can change your mood, improve your health, and even increase your intelligence. With all these good reasons to sing, I never needed much prompting, but my personal attitude received a 1000 megawatt boost when I sang a song and saved myself from electrocution.

David Francis Dayton

172

In August, 1975, I drove down a freeway at quarter to midnight, headed for the National City Steelyard where I would work my first security guard shift atop a black oil tanker. The car radio played "Get Back" by the Beatles, but I felt positive about the job and kept racing down freeway 5 toward the southwestern corner of California. Oncoming headlights dazzled my eyes, but I caught the National City Port exit just in time to switch lanes. The parking lot for the steel yard was nothing but yellow dust and gravel. I parked, crossed the street, and flashed my badge at the gatekeeper.

The gatekeeper sent me to Pier Ten, where I stood at the bottom of a mile-high structure rising up the side of the ship as though it were the Tower of Babel paired up with Moby Dick. I foolishly began thumping my feet up the steel steps, setting into motion a severe vibration. Halfway up, the shock wave caused me to grip the handrails in panic. I chanted some prayers, waited for the tremors to cease, then crawled one step at a time to the deck of the ship.

The swingshift guard hardly said goodbye; he just gave me the assignment and left the deck with a rat-a-tat-tat to the dock. For eight hours I was expected to march across the unmanned hollow boat, turning keys in loud and frightful places, and keep my sanity in a land of black holes and polar air. I sang loudly to combat the noise of the wailing machine room. I hummed while pacing the deck and tried not to stare overboard at the black abyss. Back in the guard shack, I read magazines and broke out in an occasional tune to keep myself from dozing off.

As the sun broke on the ocean's edge, I stepped out of the guard house with a fresh optimism. The mile long stretch to the stern room melted under my feet as I whistled to the seagulls above. Down the ramps I danced; I gave the machine room another chorus and turned the key. Returning from the stern, I felt intoxicated by the salt air and broke out in a rendition of Rodgers and Hammerstein's "Oh, What a Beautiful Mornin'!" from their musical play *Oklahoma*.

Screams from below stopped my voice. Workmen on the pier gestured frantically and hollered "Get back!" I understood plainly that they did not want me to touch the steel railing. A gaze over portside showed me why. During the night the ladder had rolled over a thick and frayed electric cable. The entire ladder and the side railing bristled with voltage. If the workmen on the pier had not heard my singing voice and hollered, I would have placed my bare hands on the charged steel.

The workmen removed the cable and deactivated the "live" ladder in time for the next guard to climb up and relieve me. I drove home up the freeway subdued by the near-death experience and too shaken to think. Years later, however, I realized that singing not only helped me survive that first night on the job, it saved my life.

Since that day on the job, I have sung to help friends, pass college courses, celebrate my marriage, quiet babies, and solve a number of problems. I have sung to improve my teaching, win education competitions, and to communicate local concerns to the state government. When my mood is down, when I am faced with a problem, when I need a solution, I pray.

Then God often tells me to sing.

I hope this collection of celebrated figures from three millenia who have saved lives, changed history, and witnessed miracles thanks to singing a song has encouraged you to add singing to your repertory of lifeskills.

Perhaps God will inspire you to sing and change the world, too.

And remember, only about one in a thousand people is tone deaf—unable to hear the difference between one tone and another—and most of them seem to sing loud and clear without a care. To change your life, to change the nation, to change the world with singing requires only a willingness to sing. But sometimes you might also require a song. Here is just such a song—one that summarizes the many ways you can sing and change the world.

A Song to Get You Started

(sung to the tune of "Yankee Doodle")

Sing each day and you'll be happy.
Sing to beat the daily grind.
Sing to send all fear away
The fears of heart and soul and mind.

Sing out your grief and ease your soul.
Sing out your trauma and be whole.
Sing out your heart and do your thing
And you'll be happy 'cause you sing.

Sing to block out sudden pain.
Sing to improve health.
Sing to find recovery
And overcome yourself.
Sing to keep new friends and old.
Sing to keep true love.
Sing to raise a family
With songs sent from above.

Sing to learn and
Sing to change and
Sing to make work better.
Sing to change the neighborhood
And keep the world together.

Sing to change all history.
Sing to reduce strife.
Sing to help us all recall
A man or woman's life.
Sing to save a human soul.
Sing to well inspire.
Sing to see a miracle and
Sing when you retire.

Sing on earth and sing in heaven
Let your vocals ring
You won't be singing 'cause you're happy,
You'll be happy 'cause you sing.

Resources

David E. Dayton
Submit your singing-related stories for possible publication in David's next book!
Email: David Dayton@AslanPublishing.com
Visit the author's website for regularly updated information about how you can sing and change the world.
www.singandchange.com

Aslan Publishing
2490 Black Rock Turnpike, #342, Fairfield, CT 06432
Contact the publisher for a free catalog.
Telephone: 203-372-0300; Fax: 203-374-4766
www.aslanpublishing.com

Songs of Love
A non-profit organization dedicated to creating personalized songs for chronically and terminally ill children and young adults.
www.songsoflove.org
Mailing Address:
Songs of Love Foundation
P.O.Box 750809, Forest Hills, NY 11375
E-Mail: Info@SongsOfLove.org
Telephone (toll-free): 1-800-960-SONG(7664)
Fax: 1-718-441-7372

Emissary of Light
Jimmy Twyman's workshops and concerts in the U.S. and abroad teach practical ways to bring more peace into our lives. (See "Harmonious Fact," page 45.)
http://www.emissaryoflight.com/
48 Morse Avenue, Ashland, OR 97520
Telephone: 541-482-5962

Harmony Foundation
A charitable and educational foundation affiliated
with the Society for the Preservation and
Encouragement of Barbershop Quartet Singing in
America, supporting vocal music education in our
schools and communities.
www.harmonyfoundation.org
Mailing Address: Harmony Foundation, Inc.,
6315 Harmony Lane, Kenosha, WI 53143-5199
Phone: (262) 653-8440 ext. 8447
Fax: (262) 654-5552
E-Mail: hf@spebsqsa.org

**SPEBSQSA (Society for the Preservation and
Encouragement of Barbershop Quartet Singing in
America)**
Men who want to develop as singers can learn about
voice and how to use it as part of the world's largest
all-male singing organization. Plus, plenty of
resources to encourage singing in your home,
community, and nation.
www.spebsqsa.org
E-Mail: membership@spebsqsa.org.
800-876-SING

Sweet Adelines International
A highly respected worldwide organization of women
singers committed to advancing the musical art form
of barbershop harmony through education and
performances. This independent, nonprofit music
education association is one of the world's largest
singing organizations for women.
www.sweetadelineintl.org
PO Box 470168
Tulsa OK 74147-0168
 800-992-7464
E-mail:member@sweetadelineintl.org

Black Coffee Sound Productions
Through "Performance Method Singing," Black Coffee Sound Productions seeks to promote the positive physiological and psychological benefits of singing that help unlock the creative potential, which exists in us all, to fully enjoy our life, our work, and our relationships with others.
www.blackcoffee.co.uk
25 Eden Drive, Headington
Oxford, OX3 OAB
tel: 01865 762811
fax: 01865 760444
E-mail: training@blackcoffee.co.uk

Sing Out!
A magazine whose mission is to preserve and support the cultural diversity and heritage of all traditional and contemporary folk musics, and to encourage making folk music a part of our everyday lives.
http://www.singout.org/
Sing Out!
P.O. Box 5460
Bethlehem, PA 18015
Ph: 610-865-5366
Fx: 610-865-5129
Orders: 888-SING-OUT

Dr. Carl Winter
 A serious food toxocologist with 14 years experience as a University of California faculty member, Dr. Winters has combined his background as a musician with his scientific and communication training to develop an innovative, humorous and effective approach to food safety education.
http://foodsafe.ucdavis.edu/music.html

Index

A

"A Charge to Keep I Have" 153
A Funny Thing Happened on the Way to the Forum 80
"A Hard Day's Night" 169
"A Lot of Livin' to Do" 112
"A Mighty Fortress Is Our God." 69
"A Modern Major General" 3
"Abide with Me" 50
"Abraham, Martin, and John." 146
Alamo, The 110
"All Quiet Along the Potomac Tonight" 54
All Things Must Pass 166
"All You Need Is Love" 7
"Aloha 'Oe" 91
"Amazing Grace" 39, 112, 169
"America the Beautiful" 4
"Anchors Aweigh" 40, 119
Andersen, Hans Christian 89
Andrews, Julie 71
"Anticipation" 96
Argonauts 145
Arion 55
"Arthur Murray Taught Me Dancing in a Hurry," 40
Astaire, Fred 74
Augustine of Hippo 12
Auschwitz 49
Autry, Gene 83, 162
"Ave Maria" 170
"Away in a Manger" 162
"Cielito Lindo" 134

B

Baby Burlesks *76*
"Baby, It's Cold Outside" 78

"Baby, Take a Bow" 76
Baez, Joan 102
"Ballad of Davy Crockett, The" 109
"Ballad of Joe Hill" 141
"Ballad of John Henry" 138
barbershop quartet 104
Barnum, P.T. 89
"Battle Cry of Freedom" 30
"Battle Hymn of the Republic" 17, 31
Beatles 7, 83, 169
Beethoven, Ludwig Van 121
Beltzer, John 102
Bennett, Tony 94
Berlin, Irving 115
Bernstein, Leonard 80
Black Coffee Sound Productions 83
"Blessed" 42
Bobbettes, The 171
Bofill, Dr. Rano S. 40
"Bonnie Blue Flag" 17, 31
Brando, Marlon 78
"Bridge on the River Kwai" *105*
Brooks, Tamara 42
"Brotherhood of Man" 58
Brown, Arthur 123
Browne, Jackson 40
Butterfield, Daniel 8, 14
"Butterfield's Lullaby" 15
Bye, Bye Birdie 112

C

Caedmon 25
Caesar, Julius 142
"Can the Circle Be Unbroken?" 34

"Candle in the Wind" 93
Carleston, James J. 126
Caruso, Enrico 169
Cash, Johnny 73
Cherokee Indians 125
Christians 23
Cinderella 108
Civil Rights Movement 38
Civil War 15, 17, 29, 43, 126
Clapton, Eric 133, 167
Clark, Petula 168
Claudius (Emperor) 142
"Coat of Many Colors" 47
Cochran, Eddie 83
"Come, Come Ye Saints," 39
"Comedy Tonight" 81
"Coming Around Again" 96
Coogan, Jackie 77
Cool Ones, The 168
Cornwallis, Lord Charles 28
Country Soul Of Mrs. Miller 169
Cowboy and the Senõrita 75
"Cowboy's Lullaby" 67
Crockett, Davy 109
Crosby, Bing 74, 163
Croton 29
"Curse of the Dreamer" 128
Curtis, Jamie Lee 96
Curtis, Jeffrey 3

D

"Darling Nelly Gray" 31
Davis, James Houston 159
Day, Doris 1, 64
Dean, Jimmy 146
Dear Abby 47
Debs, Eugene 73
"Der Fuehrer's Face" 170
Diana (Princess) 93
Dietrich, Marlene 76
Disney, Walt 32
"Dixie" 17, 31
"Do Not Forsake Me" 81

"Do They Know It's Christmas?
     (Feed the World)" 167
"Don't Fence Me In" 112
Double Life of Pocahontas 113
Douglas, Frederick 11
Down by the old mill stream! 5
"Down in the Arkansas" 165
"Downtown" 168
Dreiser, Theodore 128
Dresser, Paul 128
Driftwood, Jimmy 165
Dylan, Bob *97*, 145, 167

E

Ed Sullivan Show 168
Eddy, Nelson 83
"Eighth of January, The " 164
Elliot, Charlotte 120
Elzey, Kathy 4
"Empress of the Blues" 117
Ephron, Nora 96
Epstein, Brian 83
Esperian 40
Evans, Dale 74
"Everything's Coming Up
     Roses" 112

F

Fairfield Four 104
Ferdinand, Archduke Francis 19
Fisk University 129
Flowers and Trees 33
"Follow the Drinking Gourd" 10
Forman, Milos 96
Foster, Stephen 151
French and Indian War 27
Fritz, Jean 113
Funny Girl 112

G

Gandhi 39
Geldof, Bob 167

Gilbert and Sullivan 3
Gilmore, Patrick 31
"God Bless America" 4
"God Bless America"
    115, 146, 171
"God Save the King" 114
"Chapel of Love" 133
"Good King Wenceslaus" 143
"Goodnight Irene" 72
Goulet, Robert 59
Graham, Billy 120, 153
Great Depression, The 32
Gregorian Chant 52
Grisi, Giulia 89
Guys and Dolls 78
Gypsy 80, 112

H

"Hail Columbia" 17
"Hallelujah Chorus" 146, 170
Hamlish, Marvin 96
Hammerstein II, Oscar 80
Handy, W.C. 161
Hanks, Tom 96
Harrison, George 146, 166
Harrison, William Henry 160
Hassett, Buddy 132
Havens, Richie 40
Hawn, Goldie 96
Haydn, Franz Joseph 121
"He Had a Long Chain On" 165
"Heart and Soul" 55
Heartburn 96
"Here Comes Santa Claus" 162
"He's Got the Whole World in His
    Hands" 41
"He's So Fine" 166
High Noon 81
"His Eye Is on the Sparrow"
    153
Hollander, Frederick 78
Homer 144

Horace 2
*How to Succeed in Business
    Without Really Trying*
    58, 78
Howe, Julia Ward 31

I

"I Cried" 101
"I Dream of Jeanie with the
    Light Brown Hair" 151
"I Left My Heart in San Fran-
    cisco." 94
"Ida! Sweet as Apple Cider" 79
Iliad, The 144
"Impossible Dream" 57
Industrial Workers of the World
    39
"It's a Small World" 112
"Itsy Bitsy Spider" 112
"I've Been Working on the
    Railroad" 106, 133

J

Jackson, Andrew 164
Jackson, Michael 167
Jackson, Stonewall 146
Jagger, Mick 97
James, William 2
Jenkins, Florence Foster 170
"Jingle, Jangle, Jingle" 78
"John Brown's Body" 31, 146
John, Elton 93
Jones, Casey 141
Jones, Spike 170
Jubilee Singers 129
"Just a Closer Walk With Thee"
    169
"Just As I Am" 120

K

Kay, Mary 40
Kemnitz, H. Gordon 3
Key, Francis Scott 17
King David 2, 86
King, Martin Luther 38
King Richard the Lion-Hearted 22
Kingston Trio 151
Kinworthy, Eric 46, 55

L

Laine, Frankie 8, 81
Lane, Burton 78
"Last Roundup" 75
Lennon, John 7, 83
Leonard, Eddie 79
"Let the River Run" 96
"Let's Go Fly a Kite" 112
"levee hollers" 101
Levitsky, Lyuba 39
Levy, Merle 107
Lewis, C.S. 148
Life Is Beautiful 107
"Light Crust Doughboys" 158
Lili'uokalani (Queen) 91
Lilley, Joseph J. 78
Lincoln, Abraham 31
Lind, Jenny 89
Loesser, Frank 78
"Long-term Physical Effects" 96
Lully, Jean Baptiste 122
Luther, Martin 123

M

Magician's Nephew, The 148
Marks, Johnny 162
Marris, Jacque 42
"Maryland, My Maryland" 17
McCartney, Paul 83, 167
McDowall, Roddy 168

McHugh, Jimmy 78
McKinley, William 156
"Memphis Blues" 161
"Merry Widow, The" 107
Methodist Recorder 47
"Midnight Special" 73
Miller, Elva 168
Miranda, Carmen 83
"Mississippi" 145
Moses 135
Most Happy Fella 78
"Mr. Lee" 171
Mrs. Miller's Greatest Hits 169
Musical Doctor 86
"Muskrat" 36
"My Bonnie Lies over the Ocean" 83, 147
"My Country 'Tis of Thee" 115
"My Favorite Things" 112
"My Grandfather's Clock" 155
"My Happiness" 82
"My Sweet Lord" 166

N

"Navajo Happiness Song" 126
Neale, John 143
"Nearer My God to Thee" 157
Nelson, Willie 40
Newton, John 39
Nicholson, Jack 96
Ninth Symphony (Beethoven's) 121
"No Secrets" 96
"Nobody Does It Better" 96
Nothing in Common 96

O

O' Daniels, Pappy 158
O' Hara, Geoffrey 157
"O Little Town of Bethlehem," 162

Odyssey, The 144
"Oh, What a Beautiful Mornin'!"
    173
Oklahoma 173
"Old Dan Tucker" 28
"Old King Cole" 143
"On the Good Ship Lollipop" 77
Ono, Yoko 42, 54
Orpheus 145
Osmond, Donnie 170

P

"P.T. 109" 146
Palmer, Antwoine 40
Parker, Fess 112
Parton, Dolly 47
Paul and Silas 21
Peale, Norman Vincent 3
Pearl Jam 55
"Peatbog Soldiers, The" 40
"People" 112
Perfect 96
Peter Pan 112
Phillips, Sam 83
"Polly Wolly Doodle" 85
Pope Gregory 52
Potlatch Ceremony 16
"Praise the Lord and Pass the
    Ammunition," 79
Presley, Elvis 83
Prince of Egypt, The 135
Princip, Gavrilo 19
Pythagorus 29

Q

"Que Sera, Sera" 1
Questel, Mae 86

R

Ralph, Sheryl Lee 40
Rapp, Barney 64
Rescorla, Rick 54

Richard the Lion-Hearted 8
Rising, The 146
Ritchie, Lionel 167
Robbins, Jerry 81
"Rock Island Line" 73
Rodman, Dennis 55
Rogers and Hammerstein 3
Rogers, Roy 75
Rogers, Will 83
"Roll Out the Barrel" 118
Root, George F. 31
Rubin "Hurricane" Carter 145
"Rudolph the Red-Nosed
    Reindeer" 163

S

Saint Augustine 8
Santa Ana 110
Schwartz, Arthur 78
Sebastian, John 40
Seeger, Bob 97
Shakespeare, William 142
Shuckburgh, Richard 27
Sidewalks of New York, The 39
Sidorsky, Faye 49
"Silent Night" 162
Simon, Carly 96
Sinatra, Frank 78
"Singing Doctor, The" 40
"Singing in the Rain" 106
"Sixteen Tons" 36
slaves 9, 31, 60
"On a Slow Boat to China" 78
Smith, Alfred E. 39
Smith, Bessie 117
"Smoke on the Water" 39
Sondheim, Stephen 80
Songs of Love 102
sorry songs 16
Sound of Music, The 68
Springsteen, Bruce 146
Spy Who Loved Me, The 96
St. Botvid 116

St. Deogratias 116
St. Francis of Assisi 45
St. Paul 12
"Star-Spangled Banner"
        17, 31, 100
Starr, Ringo 167
"Steal Away" 24
Stewart, Jimmy 1
"Stille Nacht (Silent Night)" 19
Stonewall 113
Stradella, Allessandro 48
Streep, Meryl 96
Styne, Jule 78, 80
Swing Shift 96
Sybaris 29

T

Taking Off 96
"Taps" 15
Taylor, James 97
"Tears in Heaven" 133
"Tears on My Pillow" 162
Temple, Shirley 77
"Tennessee Stud, The" 165
"That's the Way I've Always
        Heard It Should Be." 96
"That's When Your Heartaches
        Begin" 82
"The Boy Who Never Grew Too
        Old to Comb His Mother's
        Hair" 159
"There Is No Death" 157
This Is My Life 96
"Three Coins in a Fountain" 155
Tillis, Mel 97
Tiomkin, Dmitri 81
"Tippecanoe and Tyler Too 161
Titanic 157
"Tolle lege! Tolle lege!" 12
"Tom Dooley" 151
*Traitor: The Case of Benedict
        Arnold* 113
Travis, Merle 36

Travolta, John 96
Trojan Horse 144
Trojan War, The 144
Tubman, Harriet 60
Twain, Mark 62
"Twelve Days of Christmas"
        133, 162
"Twenty Flight Rock" 83
"Twinkle, Twinkle, Little Star"
        133, 146, 165
"Two Sleepy People" 78
Twyman, James 45

U

Ulysses 144
Uncle Tom's Cabin 31
Unity Choir 40

V

Vallee, Rudy 86
Vespasian (Emperor) 23
Von Trapp, Captain 68

W

"Wait Till the Sun Shines, Nellie"
        95
"Wake Up Everybody" 101
Washington, George 28
"Waterloo" 146
Waters, Ethel 153
"We Are the World" 167
Weavers, The 73
Webb, Sheyann 38
West Side Story 80
"What Do You Do in the Infan-
        try?" 78
"What's the Matter with
        Hewitt?" 39
"When Johnny Comes Marching
        Home" 31
"When We Was Fab" 146
Where's Charley? 78

"Whisky Johnnie" 67
"White Christmas" 163
Whittier, John Greenleaf 60
Whittington, Dick 13
"Who's Afraid of the Big Bad
    Wolf?" 33
"Wild Goose" 8
Will Success Spoil Mrs. Miller?
    169
Willard, Frances E. 152
"Winkin', Blinkin', and Nod" 96
Winter, Carl 105
Working Girl 96
World Trade Center
    54, 101, 146
"World Turned Upside Down" 28

Y

"Yankee Doodle"
    17, 31, 134, 175
Yellow Submarine 7
"You Are My Sunshine" 159
"You Can Do It" 108
"You Can Fly" 112
"You're So Vain" 96

PUBLISHING

Our Mission

Aslan Publishing offers readers a window to the soul via well-crafted and practical self-help books, inspirational books, and modern day parables. Our mission is to publish books that uplift one's mind, body, and spirit.

Living one's spirituality in business, relationships, and personal growth is the underlying purpose of our publishing company, and the meaning behind our name Aslan Publishing. We see the word "Aslan" as a metaphor for living spiritually in a physical world.

Aslan means "lion" in several Middle Eastern languages. The most famous "Aslan" is a lion in The Chronicles of Narnia by C. S. Lewis. In these stories, Aslan is the Messiah, the One who appears at critical points in the story in order to point human beings in the right direction. Aslan doesn't preach, he acts. His actions are an inherent expression of who he is.

We hope to point the way toward joyful, satisfying and healthy relationships with oneself and with others. Our purpose is to make a real difference in our readers' everyday lives.

About the Author

David Dayton is a Mentor Teacher at Bowling Green Charter School, part of the Sacramento City Unified School District in California. A Sacramento County "Teacher of the Year," he teaches Kindergarten for the district and English to second-language learners at Sacramento City College. David combines his singing, writing and speaking talents to entertain, inform and persuade students, educators, parents, boards of education and even an occasional California State Senate gathering.

David lives in Sacramento with his wife, Karin, and eight children. His goal is to speak and sing to organizations across the nation and around the world about the power of positive singing.

Send David your favorite stories related to singing. Your singing saga might be included in his next book!

EMAIL: DavidDayton@AslanPublishing.com

WEBSITE: www.singandchange.com

Send David your personal stories about singing!

Has singing ever helped you...

...solve a problem?
...recover from illness?
...achieve success?
...change your life for the better?

Email your true story, in 600 words or less, to:
DavidDayton@AslanPublishing.com
Include complete contact information.
If selected, your story will be published in David's
next book about how singing can change the world!

Hannah Dayton

Titles Published by Aslan

Aslan PUBLISHING

*The Candida Control
Cookbook What You
Should Know And What
You Should Eat To
Manage Yeast Infections*
by Gail Burton
$14.95
ISBN 0-944031-67-6

*Workout for the Soul: 8 Steps
to Inner Fitness*
by Chrissie Blaze
$14.95
ISBN 0-944031-90-0

*The Gift of Wounding:
Finding Hope & Heart
in Challenging
Circumstances*
by Andre Auw Ph.D.
$13.95
ISBN 0-944031-79-X

*How Loving Couples Fight:
12 Essential Tools for
Working Through the Hurt*
by James L Creighton Ph.D.
$16.95
ISBN 0-944031-71-4

*Intuition Workout: A
Practical Guide To
Discovering & Developing
Your Inner Knowing*
by Nancy Rosanoff
$12.95
ISBN 0-944031-14-5

*The Joyful Child:
A Sourcebook of Activities
and Ideas for Releasing
Children's Natural Joy*
by Peggy Jenkins Ph.D.
$16.95
ISBN 0-944031-66-8

Solstice Evergreen: The History, Folklore & Origins of the Christmas Tree
2nd ed by Sheryl Karas
$14.95
ISBN 0-944031-75-7

What Happened to the Prince I Married: Spiritual Healing for a Wounded Relationship
by Sirah Vettese Ph.D.
$14.95
ISBN 0-944031-76-5

If You Want to be Rich & Happy Don't Go to School: Ensuring Lifetime Security for Yourself & Your Children
by Robert T. Kiyosaki
$15.95
ISBN 0-944031-59-5

More Aslan Titles

Facing Death, Finding Love: The Healing Power Of Grief & Loss in One Family's Life
by Dawson Church, $10.95; ISBN 0-944031-31-5

Gentle Roads to Survival: Making Self-Healing Choices in Difficult Circumstances
by Andre Auw Ph.D. $10.95; ISBN 0-944031-18-8

Lynn Andrews in Conversation with Michael Toms
edited by Hal Zina Bennett, $8.95; ISBN 0-944031-42-0

Argument With An Angel
by Jan Cooper, $11.95; ISBN 0-944031-63-3

To order any of Aslan's titles send a check or money order for the price of
the book plus Shipping & Handling

Book Rate $3 for 1st book.; $1.00 for each additional book
First Class $4 for 1st book; $1.50 for each additional book

Send to: ***Aslan Publishing***
2490 Black Rock Turnpike # 342
Fairfield CT 06825

To receive a current catalog: please call (800) 786–5427 or (203) 372–0300
E-mail us at: **info@aslanpublishing.com**
Visit our website at **www.aslanpublishing.com**

*Our authors are available for seminars, workshops, and lectures. For further information
or to reach a specific author, please call or email Aslan Publishing.*